HAUNTED
LIVERPOOL 3

The author would like to thank Liverpool Central Library for the use of their microfilm and microfiche machines. Thanks also to Alec McKie for the use of his database system.

First published 1998
This edition published 2003

Published by The Bluecoat Press, Liverpool
Book design by March Design, Liverpool
Printed by The Universities Press, Belfast

ISBN 1 872568 51 3

Tom Slemen
HAUNTED
LIVERPOOL 3

The Bluecoat Press

Contents

Introduction

A couple of years ago, that sober, errorless register of facts and figures, the *Guinness Book of Records*, stated that Britain is the most haunted country in the world, with more ghosts per square mile than any other nation. Why this is so is anybody's guess, as there are other regions of the world which have a longer and bloodier history than ours.

The ghost is an archetype found in all cultures of the human race. Hindus believe in the Pretas, evil ghosts that fight for the possession of a living body and Celts have their Banshee, who announces an imminent death with her frightful wailings. Nigerians say that there are haunted trees which are inhabited by the spirits of the dead and the Matumba of central Africa will vouch for the existence of malevolent ghosts which can only be combated with water. The Algonquin Indians of Canada have an unquestioning belief in the ghosts of their ancestors and regularly give the spirits offerings of food and water, while in the mythology of ancient China, there are allusions to evil phantoms that were known as the 'Kuei'. These nasty entities were said to roam in search of victims to take their place in hell.

Ghosts are even mentioned in the Bible's Old Testament. In the Book of Job 4: 14-16, there is a mention of a hair-raising encounter: "Fear came upon me, and trembling, which made all my bones to shake. Then a spirit passed before my face, the hair of my flesh stood up. It stood still, but I could not discern the form thereof ..."

Another supernatural incident takes place in the Book of Samuel, when the Witch of Endor conjures up the shade of the dead prophet Samuel so Saul can converse with him.

Ghosts then, are by no means a contemporary phenomenon and are not restricted to any particular race. The ghost stories and grisly narratives contained in this book are the result of years of research in the newspaper archives of Liverpool's Central Library, where I scanned miles of microfilm in search of supernatural reports with a local flavour. I also read a mountain of books, many of which were out of print, on the folklore and legends of Merseyside and Cheshire.

However, the most interesting source of unusual stories I tapped into was the local populace. For eighteen months, Billy Butler, a presenter at Merseyside's independent local radio station, kindly gave me a regular thirty minute slot talking about local hauntings, grisly Victorian murders and unsolved mysteries of local history on his popular breakfast radio programme. The response from the listening public was unexpected and phenomenal. There was a deluge of mail and phone calls from people of all walks of life, from the dustman to the doctor, all eager to tell me their strange tales. There were also many intriguing enquiries. People asked me if I'd heard of the 'Spectre of Smithdown Road' who is regularly mistaken for a living person, or of the spooky jukebox that plays prophetic songs, or of the girl who married a dead man, or of the crawling ghost known as 'Resurrection Mary', and so on.

I was literally bombarded with such stories for eighteen months and I ended up sleeping with the light on each night! I still contacted now, and although I can sleep in the dark, I still occasionally get goosebumps when I recall some of the stories I have researched for this book. Even as I type these words, I have the sneaking suspicion that I am not alone in my study ...

Tom Slemen

The Sad Spectre of Smithdown Road

The following spooky incident happened in Liverpool in the early 1990s and was even reported in the *Liverpool Echo*.

One morning at around four o'clock, a twenty-four year-old man named Alan was walking home from a pub in Smithdown Road. There had been a stay-behind at the pub because the landlady was celebrating her recent engagement, and Alan felt quite drunk. He was walking near Sefton General Hospital, which is situated in Smithdown Road, when he noticed a girl standing on the pavement near a bus stop. She wore an incredibly short dress with a revealing top and had long blonde hair. She looked about nineteen or twenty and Alan assumed she was waiting for a taxi. She just stood there shivering, stamping her high heels because of the cold.

"You're not on the game are you?" Alan joked, attempting to chat her up.

The girl smiled and shook her head.

"I'm dead cold," she complained.

Alan saw his opportunity and he took off his denim jacket and offered it to her.

"Who said chivalry was dead?" he responded as the girl took it and put it on. Three sizes too large, it looked ridiculous on her.

"Waiting for a taxi?" Alan asked.

"No. Waiting for my boyfriend," she replied looking down Smithdown Road, squinting as she looked intently for a sign of him.

Alan's heart sank. He thought, "Just my luck. She's going with someone."

"He does my head in, you know; I've been waiting here for ages. He always does this," added the girl.

"Does what?" Alan asked.

"Says he's gonna pick me up and then doesn't turn up," she replied.

"Get another boyfriend who's more reliable then." Alan said, giving her the hint.

"Nah, I love Tony," she answered smiling.

"But does he love you?" asked Alan cheekily.

"Oh, I suppose he's not coming," moaned the girl, looking worried. "I wonder if something's happened to him?"

"No, he's probably with some girl. We fellas are only human y'know, despite our alien appearance," laughed Alan, trying to cheer her up.

The girl tutted and walked along. Alan walked with her, admiring her legs and her figure. She was a real stunner. "What's your name?" he asked

"Jodie," she replied.

"Ooh, Jodie Foster eh? My name's Alan. My mates call me Alan Ladd."

Jodie smiled and walked on. Then she bowed her head as if she was going to cry and ran into Toxteth Park Cemetery.

Alan surmised she was either going to be sick because she had been drinking too much, or that she was going to powder her nose. He wanted to relieve himself too, after all the drinking.

After about ten minutes, Alan shouted into the darkness of the cemetery, "Jodie! Jodie? Are you okay?"

As he crept past the gravestones, there was no sign of her. He expected to find her on the ground, out cold with drinking, yet she had not appeared drunk. By now it was almost dawn and the sky was getting paler by the minute. "You had me worried there girl," he called out aloud as he thought he saw her, but it was his denim jacket, draped over a gravestone. "What's she playing at?" he mumbled. Then he saw Jodie's face, on the gravestone. A photograph of Jodie to be precise and, underneath the oval photograph, the inscription said she had been born in 1970 and had died tragically in 1990, just six months earlier. Alan was terrified by now. He ran out of the cemetery into Smithdown Road and did not stop running until he reached his home almost a mile away. He fell down on his doorstep when he got home and his trembling hand inserted the key in the Yale lock.

A week later, he told his two best friends about the ghost he had tried to chat up and Brian, one of his mates, recalled that his sister had been a friend of Jodie's. Brian then told the sad story. Jodie had arranged to meet her boyfriend near the bus stop at Sefton General Hospital on Smithdown Road. Jodie had not known that she had a hole in her heart and she collapsed and died. Although people tried to help by taking her to the hospital, there was nothing that anyone

9

could do. Jodie's parents phoned her boyfriend and told him the bad news, he was so upset that he vowed he would never drive up Smithdown Road again. To this day, he never drives near the road.

On the following night, Alan and Brian walked to Jodie's grave and placed a bouquet of carnations on it. Brian's sister said carnations had been her favourite flowers. As the lads walked away from the cemetery, Alan glanced back and was certain he saw Jodie waving. The ghost is still occasionally seen by motorists driving up Smithdown Road in the early hours of the morning. As recently as 1996, a taxi driver stopped for the girl at three in the morning and when he looked around, the pavement was deserted.

Rings on her Fingers

The following spooky tale is one of the earliest recorded ghost stories in the North West and allegedly took place in Liverpool in the autumn of 1826.

In October 1826, a fifty-six-year-old Liverpool pawnbroker named William Poole buried his wife Rose, who had died from typhoid. The neighbours of the pawnbroker, who lived in a lane off Dale Street, thought it was disgraceful that he was already flirting with young women in the local tavern so soon after the death of Mrs Poole. Only a fortnight after the funeral of his wife, Poole was already seriously involved with a pretty young girl named Katie Holland. Katie was only seventeen and had just broken up with her boyfriend, so she sought solace in the arms of the lecherous pawnbroker.

By the end of November, Katie discovered she was pregnant with Poole's child and so the couple married a week later at St George's Church, which once stood in Derby Square.

Poole was having quite a hard time financially and was concerned that he might not be able to afford a decent wedding ring for his bride. However, on the day of the wedding, a fabulous thick gold band, encrusted with an array of sparkling sapphires and rubies was put on Katie's finger. Later, when the couple honeymooned in North Wales, Mr Poole bestowed five other breathtaking gold rings upon his beautiful young bride.

After a fortnight, the newly-married couple returned from their honeymoon to Liverpool. Poole carried Katie over the threshold of his house and up four flights of stairs to the four poster bed. The couple were tired by the long journey home and soon fell asleep.

About four o'clock in the morning, Katie awoke and saw moonlight shining through the bedroom window. She closed her eyes and stretched out her left arm but as she did so, she felt icy cold fingers grasping her outstretched hand. Katie glanced sideways and to her horror, saw a woman dressed in what seemed to be a white shroud. The woman looked as if she was dead. A thin layer of bluish-white skin lightly covered her skeletal face. Katie thought the ghoul's dark, prominent eyes seemed sad as she fought to free her hand. Katie tried to scream but her throat had closed up with fear. The corpse-like woman suddenly muttered, "Give me my rings back ... give me them!" as her bony fingers tried to pull off the wedding ring and the so-called friendship rings.

Katie suddenly managed to let out a scream that startled her husband from his slumber. William Poole awoke with fright as Katie turned to him, hugging him as she trembled. The ghostly figure had disappeared.

Katie told William about the strange gruesome apparition and he said she had had a nightmare but Katie knew it was not a dream and insisted on sleeping with lit candles placed about the room.

The following afternoon, while William was at work, Katie was alone in the house. She was washing clothes in the kitchen, when she heard a whining sound behind her. She turned around and saw the same ghoulish figure standing in the hall with its arms stretched out, coming towards her. The figure was whimpering and pleading, "Please give me my rings back."

Katie ran out of the back door into the arms of the Reverend Richard Kelly, the clergyman who had married her and William. Having listened to her account of the strange woman who was haunting her, the vicar took Katie to his house, which was annexed to St George's Church and gave her a drink to steady her. As she told the story once more, he gazed at her in deep thought. After much contemplation, he suddenly stood up.

"I hope I'm wrong. Come with me," he said, and he led Katie out into the churchyard. He threaded his way through the gravestones until he came to the grave of Poole's deceased wife, Rose. The grave had obviously been disturbed, so the Reverend summoned two burly grave-diggers to exhume her body. They opened the coffin and young Katie fainted when she noticed that the decomposing corpse in the coffin was identical to the ghost in the shroud which had visited her twice. Furthermore, the rings were missing from the hands of the corpse.

When William Poole was confronted by the Reverend Kelly, he started to sob and admitted he had stolen the rings from his dead wife to give to his new bride. Katie left her despicable husband even after he had returned the rings to his wife's coffin.

Ironically, a year later, two grave-robbers named Robert Tryer and John Woods ransacked the grave of Rose Poole and stole her rings and jewellery. The grave robbers were captured and transported to Australia, but the rings of Rose Poole were never found, although there were rumours that they were purchased by a family with the widespread surname of Jones. Perhaps the rings are still being passed down through the generations to their unwitting descendants.

The Ashes

In 1985, a seventy-six-year-old pensioner named Maud lost her husband Bill when he died of cancer. The couple, who lived in the Merseyside area, were inseparable and Bill knew that when he died, Maud would feel very lost and alone. During the couple's last conversation, Maud said life without him would be unbearable. Bill replied, "Keep your chin up love, because if there is a life after this one, I'll be there looking over you night and day. When the worst happens, just carry on and pretend I'm in the room with you. Call me by my old familiar name."

Bill was cremated and Maud kept his ashes in an ornamental urn which she kept by her bed. Each night, before she switched off the light, she would say goodnight to the urn. She knew it was silly, but it was her way of coping without Bill.

In the Christmas of 1985, Maud went into town to do some shopping. She entered a large department store and during the shopping trip, she went to the ladies toilet. Instead of hanging her handbag on a hook, she put it on the floor. Within seconds, someone had reached under the toilet door and snatched her bag. That bag had contained her pension book, four hundred pounds in cash that she had saved to buy her grandchildren Christmas presents, her late husband's wallet and wedding ring, and a cash card along with her PIN number, which she had foolishly scrawled on a piece of paper because she never could remember the four-digit code.

Maud reported the theft to the manager of the store and the police, who gave the unfortunate pensioner a lift home in a squad car. Because she did not have her keys, a little boy in the street had to go through the bathroom window to open the door for her.

Maud went upstairs to the bedroom and sobbed. She held the urn containing Bill's ashes and hugged it as she cried.

"Oh, Bill. How could someone do this to me? Help me Bill," she wept.

The following morning the phone rang, and Maud answered it. It was the manager of the department store where her handbag had been stolen. He said he had found the handbag intact and that nothing was missing. She only had to collect and sign for the handbag. What's more, the manager said he would give Maud a free Christmas hamper because of the trauma she'd been through.

Maud was elated. She used the money a sympathetic neighbour had given her to take a taxi to the department store, but when she arrived the manager was baffled. He said, "I didn't call you and no one has reported finding your handbag. Someone must be pulling your leg. I'm so sorry."

Maud said, "But how would they know my telephone number?"

"Oh dear," said the manager of the department store as he looked at Maud, "I hope I'm wrong, but the person who phoned you could be the one who stole your bag. Perhaps he told you to come here just to get you out the house so he and his associates can empty it because I assume they have the keys. They were probably watching you as you left the house."

"Oh no!" Maud cried, starting to shake. The manager ran to the nearest phone and alerted the police. By the time the police got to the house, the robbers had already been and had taken everything of value. Jewellery, the video, the television, everything that was worth something was gone, even the phone. Maud was led to the bedroom to see the mess the robbers had left and to her complete horror she saw that the ornamental china urn containing her husband's ashes had also been taken. She felt faint when she saw the urn missing and collapsed onto the bed. She was later taken to hospital and, because of high blood pressure and reoccurring dizzy spells, she woke up several times during the night in the hospital.

At around three in the morning, Maud awoke and saw her husband Bill standing at the foot of the bed. He was surrounded by a silvery light and was smiling at her.

"Bill, is that you?" Maud gasped, raising her hands to the vision of her late husband.

"Yes dear, everything's going to be just fine. Go to sleep. Everything will be okay in the morning, now go to sleep," said Bill, in a very calm manner.

"But Bill, you're ..." Maud stammered, unable to finish the sentence.

"I know, but I'm waiting somewhere very near and I still feel very much alive. I gave those cowards who took your bag quite a scare. Now go to sleep. You need rest," he told her and started to fade away. Suddenly, there was no one at the foot of the bed anymore. Maud closed her eyes, feeling much better after seeing Bill and slept soundly.

At ten in the morning, two policemen called into the ward and told Maud some strange news. The criminals who had taken her handbag and robbed her house were a woman named Jackie and her boyfriend Giles. They had confessed to the robbery and the housebreaking after something strange had happened to them.

Giles had opened the burial urn and was peering into it with his girlfriend and laughing, when some of the ashes shot out of the urn and burnt Giles in the eyes. Jackie washed her boyfriend's eyes, but he still could not see. In the end, she took him to the hospital and the doctors in casualty asked him how he got the ash in his eyes. Giles was in agony and he made a confession telling the medical staff the whole heinous story. The police were called in and the couple were charged.

Then Maud remembered the vision of her husband in the wee small hours and how he told her that he had scared the people who took her handbag and ransacked her home. The incident was investigated by the Psychical Research Society and, as is usual in these cases, the whole episode was filed away for posterity. It took three months for the robber's eyesight to return and an ophthalmologist who treated him said he could not explain the blindness.

Maud was later reunited with the urn and still talks to it on a regular basis.

A Marriage Made in Hell

The following story allegedly happened in Liverpool in the 1960s. There are many fanciful versions of the tale that have been circulating the city for many years but this is the original version. It is the story of a young girl who was forever dreaming about marriage.

In the mid-1960s Liverpool, a young woman named Collette worked in a textile factory near Wood Street in the city centre. Collette was a pretty but introverted girl, who had no real friends at the factory. She just kept to herself and hardly ever spoke to the eight other women who worked with her.

Each day at lunch, the girls from the factory would go to a cafe in Bold Street but Collette never went with them. Instead, she went to a kiosk round the corner to buy cigarettes and would walk up Bold Street, window shopping. She always seemed to be in a world of her own. Every day, she would gaze through the window of a certain shop that had expensive wedding dresses on display. She spent almost all of her lunch-hour staring at these dresses in a dreamy state. One of her workmates named Chrissy used to see Collette wistfully gazing at the wedding gowns and she used to wonder what the lonely girl was thinking of.

Collette kept a diary and recorded all of her most intimate thoughts in her little black book. She used to fantasise over various film stars and wonder what type of man her future husband would be. She always imagined he would be tall, dark and very handsome.

Collette was attractive but she seemed to have difficulty meeting members of the opposite sex. One night at her flat in Huskisson Street, an old black woman named Mona who was a neighbour heard Collette sobbing. Mona tapped on Collette's door and asked if she was alright. Collette came to the door in a dreadful state. Mona took her down to her basement flat and gave the girl a cup of tea. Collette said she had asked a boy out and he had turned her down. Mona said he must have been a fool and boosted the girl's confidence by saying she was very pretty and that boys were ten-a-penny.

About an hour later, as Collette left Mona's flat, she met a sinister old man on the stairs who had only just moved into the flats. She only knew him as Mr Rose and he appeared to be very strange. He always dressed in black and was always accompanied by a black cat.

"Hello, Mr Rose," Collette said, as she passed the old man on the stairs.

"If we meet on the stairs, we'll never meet in heaven," said Mr Rose, joking about an old superstition. Then in a serious tone he told her, "Collette, I couldn't help overhearing you and Mona before."

"Yes?" exclaimed Collette and she began to blush.

"I think I can help you. Come on," said the old man, and he beckoned the girl to come into his flat. Collette felt very nervous, and when she went into the old man's flat it was very dark. There were dusty old books on astrology and the occult everywhere. The old man even had a crystal ball on the table. He told her to sit at a table and handed her a piece of paper.

"That's a pact with the Devil," he explained in a matter-of-fact way and offered her a pen.

Collette grinned and looked at the words scrawled on the paper. They seemed to be in Latin and were so small, she could not make head nor tail of them. "What does it say?" she asked.

"In return for your soul, you can have anything you desire. Just write your name at the bottom of the page," said Mr Rose and he uncapped an old fountain pen and handed it to the girl.

"I don't believe in all that. There is no Devil," said Collette.

"I know, yes," said Mr Rose, "but just sign it anyway, go on."

"But ..." stammered the girl.

"No buts. Just do it! Do it! Go on. You want to," said the old man, hypnotically staring at her.

Collette signed it and laughed. "I want to marry a man who's tall dark and handsome," she wished out loud, then left the room, giggling and trotted up the stairs to her flat.

On the following day during her lunchbreak, Collette was gazing in the window of the shop again, focusing on the beautiful satin and lace wedding gown. Suddenly, she saw a face reflected in the window.

It was a tall dark-haired man with a handsome face. He was looking over her shoulder and his sudden presence naturally startled the girl.

"Oooh! Who are you?" exclaimed Collette.

As she looked at the man, he grinned and he looked so dashing, but the pupils of his eyes suddenly burned with a dim red light.

Collette stumbled back in fear against the window. The figure then glided towards her without walking.

"Don't be afraid Collette. I want to marry you. I want you. You made your promise to me," said the weird stranger.

Collette let out a scream and ran up Bold Street in a state of terror. When she got home she barricaded herself in her flat and hid under a table.

At eight that night, the stranger called at her house in Huskisson Street. Collette looked through the window and saw he was in the street below with a brown paper parcel. She screamed, "Don't let him in!", but the old woman Mona let him enter. He tapped on Collette's door, saying, "Let me in Collette, I love you. I'm your future husband," but suddenly turned nasty, shouting, "Let me in, damn you!"

Then there was silence.

Collette sat up all night drinking coffee and listening to her radio. As soon as morning came, she planned to leave her flat for good and she started writing down all the strange events that had happened in her diary. However, Collette never got to finish her entry for that day she dropped dead of a tremendous heart attack.

Mona found the girl the next day with her eyes wide open, filled with terror. When the police called at the flat, they saw that someone had left a brown-paper parcel on the landing outside the girl's flat. What they saw was bizarre: it was a black silk and satin wedding dress, just like the one in the window in Bold Street, but in black. When Mona read the dead girl's diary, she shuddered and decided to confront old Mr Rose, the man who had persuaded Collette to sign a pact with the Devil. But Mr Rose's flat was completely empty. Nobody had seen him leave and nobody ever saw that old man again.

Spooky Jukebox

The following story may seem far-fetched but it was reported in local newspapers and featured on a local BBC news programme.

In the mid-1980s, an electrician was trying to fix a troublesome jukebox at a pub in northern Liverpool, when he accidentally touched the live circuit board and suffered a fatal heart attack after being electrocuted. The barmaid, Lorraine, let out a scream when she saw the electrician collapse and was shaken by the tragedy. Around a fortnight after his death, strange things started to occur in the pub. The centre of these weird events was the jukebox.

A lorry driver went in one lunchtime for a pint of cider and a pie and as he sipped his drink he went over to the jukebox and keyed in a Bruce Springsteen song called 'Dancin' in the Dark'. However, the jukebox played 'Heat of the Moment' by a group called Asia.

Three hours later, the lorry driver was burned alive when his HGV, which was carrying tons of vegetable oil, jackknifed near Knutsford, hit the central reservation of the motorway and burst into flames. One of the drinkers who heard the tragic news on the radio in the pub was the first to connect the subject of the jukebox's song 'Heat of the Moment' and the lorry driver's death, but his mates said it was just a morbid coincidence.

A woman named Mary went into the pub one evening and walked to the jukebox. She pressed the buttons to play Michael Jackson's 'One Day In Your Life' but, instead, a golden oldie came on called 'Viva Espania'. The woman laughed at the jukebox. The following day her husband won a competition in a magazine, two weeks in Spain for two people. They were both soon holidaying in Benidorm.

That same week, a middle-aged man named Bob went into the pub to play darts with his mates. He went to the jukebox, inserted his money, then selected an old Beatles song. Instead of 'Hey Jude', 'If You Leave Me Now', a song by the American group 'Chicago' started to play. Bob shrugged and went back to playing darts. A few minutes later, Bob's brother walked into the pub with tears in his eyes and broke the bad news that Bob's wife had just been knocked down and killed by a drunken driver.

By now, the regular drinkers in the pub were starting to see the connection between the songs on the jukebox and the corresponding incidents that were happening to the customers when they played the jukebox. The drinkers told the landlady of the pub to replace the spooky jukebox, but she just said they were all crazy and that there was nothing wrong with the machine. She put some coins in to prove her point and selected a song by an old favourite group of hers, Pickety Witch. Instead, a song by David Bowie came on the jukebox called 'Ashes to Ashes'. The drinkers all warned the landlady that the pub would probably burn down. There was no fire but the outcome was much more sinister.

The landlady went to Woolwich in London to see her ex-husband who had been fighting cancer. His common-law wife had been looking after him and the landlady asked her where her ex-husband was. The woman laughed coldly and pointed to an urn containing the man's ashes; he had died a month back and had instructed his partner to have him cremated. The landlady fainted. When she regained consciousness, she accused her ex-husband's partner of being an ignorant and cold-hearted woman and returned to Liverpool.

The landlady immediately had the haunted jukebox removed. According to eight witnesses including an off-duty policeman, as the unplugged jukebox was being carried into a van, it started to play music for about ten seconds, even though it was no longer connected to the mains. The song it played was very fitting indeed: it was 'Thankyou for the Music' by Abba ...

A Labour of Lust

The following strange tale allegedly occurred in the little village of Ambleford, near Gresford, in Cheshire. Sadly, the village no longer exists, but records show that Ambleford was a very prosperous and close-knit community. One warm summer evening in 1740, a beautiful gypsy girl named Becky was waiting for her boyfriend, a blacksmith's son named Robin Tabley, in a meadow outside the village. The eighteen year-old gypsy girl was said to be a real beauty and turned the heads of every man in the village. Yet she only had eyes for young Robin, who was just fifteen.

Robin's father was a drunken bully who banned his son from seeing any gypsy girls, but Robin still met Becky in secret whenever he could and intended to run away with her to be married at Gretna Green.

On this particular summer night, a huge full moon loomed over the countryside and the gypsy girl felt there was something evil afoot. She waited for Robin for ages but the boy was nowhere to be seen. Robin had been caught sneaking out of his bedroom window by his father and had received a hiding with the strap.

At around one in the morning, just as a barn owl hooted, a sinister figure came out of the nearby woods and approached the gypsy girl. He was just a shadow because his back was turned to the moon. The figure called out, "Becky, come hither, girl."

The voice sounded vaguely familiar, so Becky walked over to the man. Then she saw he wore a mask like a highwayman but, by then, it was too late. The man pounced on her as Becky turned to run but tripped over her long dress. Within a heartbeat, the man was on top of her. He pinned her down with his muscular arms and forced kisses on her face, neck and breasts. Becky tried to scream but the man hit her across the face three times and produced a small flintlock pistol. He pressed the barrel against the frightened girl's bosom and whispered, "If you cry out, I'll shoot you through the heart."

The girl quivered with fear as the attacker dug the barrel hard against her cleavage and gritted his teeth. The man then pulled up the girl's dress and what followed was a cowardly sexual assault. The man then got to his feet, pulled up his trousers and ran off into the moonlit woods. Becky just lay there, collapsed, on the floor, sobbing.

Becky never told Robin about the attack. However, she did go to her old gypsy grandmother, a woman named Ursula, and told her about the rape. Ursula dangled a strange-looking pendulum over Becky's abdomen then muttered some spell. She then smiled and said, "You will bear no child. No seed has taken root."

Becky started to cry with relief and held her grandmother's hand. Ursula suddenly started murmuring what seemed to be the words of a hex and she seemed very angry as she cast the spell. Then the old woman explained what her magic would do.

"Do you know what couvade is, girl?"

Becky shook her head. She was not yet well versed in the occult lore of the Romany people.

Old Ursula explained: "Sometimes a man goes through labour pains when his wife is suffering in her pregnancy. That is known as couvade. It only happens when the man has been lustful. If a man who loves his wife dearly impregnates her, he suffers no such pains. I tell you truly Becky, the man who ravished you shall have labour pains as if he were giving birth to the Devil."

Becky was intrigued by her grandmother's words. The months went by, and Robin and Becky courted through the Autumn and Winter. Finally, Robin proposed to the girl and offered her a simple golden ring. Becky said she loved him but told him that she thought they were too young to marry. Robin insisted that he was old enough and pleaded for her to say yes to his question but the girl was not sure. Robin then suggested running away to Gretna Green but neither of them had any money, so they walked along the lonely country lane in the snow, holding hands and feeling depressed. Suddenly, they saw a riderless horse wandering around further up the lane in a clearing. On the floor was a man who looked as if he was dying. Robin instantly recognised him as the vicar of Ambleford, the Reverend Morley. Robin and Becky ran up to him and asked him what the matter was.

"Help me, I feel as if I've been poisoned!" said the Reverend, and he curled up and squirmed about.

Robin bent down and saw something very strange. The Reverend – who was a rather thin man – had a round bulging belly. This round mass actually seemed to move in and out as the vicar screamed. Robin naturally recoiled in horror at the sight of the inflating stomach. Becky recognised the voice of her attacker and realised that it had been the Reverend Morley who had molested her on that moonlit night. Now he was suffering the labour pains of childbirth, thanks to Ursula's spell.

When Morley set eyes on the gypsy girl, he had guilt written on his face, and he cried, "You've had a curse of couvade put upon me, wench. Please break this spell! Please. Here! Have all my money!"

The reverend took out his full purse and threw it at Becky. The girl took it and pulled Robin away by the arm. She explained what Morley had done. Robin was furious and wanted to harm the priest but Becky simply said, "Let him suffer, that's enough," and the couple left

Ambleford with the money and went to be married at Gretna Green.

The couple settled in Carlisle and prospered. They had many children and, one day, out of curiosity, Robin returned to Ambleford in disguise. He asked the new vicar what had become of Morley. The new vicar of Ambleford church told a strange tale. He said Morley's stomach had swollen up so large he had become stuck between the gateposts of his house. Several people struggled to get him free but the agony was too much so he confessed that he had raped a gypsy girl named Becky. He said that the girl had never been seen again and neither had her sweetheart, a blacksmith's son named Robin Tabley. The authorities accused him of murdering the couple and imprisoned him but before the trial began, the vicar was found dead on the floor of his cell. He was surrounded by blood and water and the strange bulge in his stomach had gone. One of the guards noticed something very peculiar. There were little tiny footprints of blood in the cell which led away from the body. These footprints were very strange because they only had three toes.

"There was a lot of talk about it in the village," said the vicar, "and some said it looked as if the evil Reverend Morley had given birth to a devil ..."

The Bloke

The following incident took place at a certain house in Liverpool in 1985. The ghost in the story is still active but as the people who currently live in the haunted house are not yet aware that they have a ghost on their premises, the street cannot be mentioned in the story. This ghost could be in the house next door to you or it could even be in your house. However, don't worry if Jarvis is with you now, because he's a very friendly and helpful ghost.

In the late summer of 1985, a twelve year-old boy named Alex was sitting having breakfast with his family when, suddenly, a jar of marmalade in front of him slid a few inches across the tablecloth, startling everyone. The boy's parents and seven year-old sister were naturally quite astonished, but Alex just smirked and whispered, "Stop it, Jarvis".

His mother's mouth dropped open and she looked at the

marmalade jar, then looked at Alex.

"How did you do that?" she asked.

"I didn't, Mum," protested Alex. "Jarvis did it."

"Who?" asked Alex's father, who had been reading the newspaper.

"The bloke from upstairs," Alex replied, and ate his cornflakes.

"Eh? What bloke, son?" Alex's father was very intrigued by his son's comments.

Alex had a lot of explaining to do. He began, "Well, Dad, this bloke comes into my room at night. He tells me stories sometimes and he looks as if he's a ghost, 'cos you can see through him. He's like a fuzzy shadow and I told him that I'd never tell anyone about him. He said he's French and his name's Jarvis something. I can't remember his second name. It isn't Smith or anything."

Alex's parents looked at each other, not knowing whether to laugh or be concerned. Alex's sister, Kelly, giggled and put her hand to her mouth. She said, "Stop telling porkies, Alex. There's no bloke upstairs in your room. Stop giving him pocket money, Dad, 'cos he's telling lies."

That night, Alex's Dad left his bedroom to go to the toilet and, as he walked past his son's bedroom, he heard a conversation. He thought his son was talking in his sleep, so he opened the door to look in and saw Alex sitting up in bed with his bedside lamp on. At the bottom of the bed there was an outline of a shady figure which vanished as he looked at it. Alex's Dad slapped the light switch to turn the light on and looked in complete disbelief at the space at the end of Alex's bed where the ghostly figure had been seconds before. He grabbed his son by the arm and yanked him out of bed, then dragged him to his bedroom, where he closed the door and put a chair against it. Alex's mum woke up and asked what all the noise was about. Her husband was astonished.

"I saw it! I saw the ghost. He's bloody right! There is a ghost in his room! I can't believe what I saw."

"Oh calm down, Dad. It's okay. Jarvis is alright, honest."

"I'm frightened," said Alex's mother and she got up and turned the light on.

"Shall we stay over at your Mum's?" Alex's father asked his wife.

"Are you sure you weren't dreaming, love?" Alex's mother asked her husband.

"I know what I saw!" he shouted and suddenly there was a rapping at the door. Alex's parents jumped. His mum let out a scream.

"Mummy," said a girl's voice. It was little Kelly. She had woken up with all the noise.

Kelly's parents opened the door and took her into their room. "It's alright, Kelly. You can sleep with Mummy and Daddy tonight," said Kelly's mum.

"I'm tired Dad," complained Alex. "I want to sleep in my own bed."

"No, you can't. There's a you-know-what in there," replied his father in a harsh voice. He couldn't mention the word 'ghost' in case he scared Kelly, but he seemed to be the most terrified. The whole family slept in the same double bed and hardly got any sleep. Throughout the night, Alex's parents kept jumping at every little sound.

The following day, when the kids were at school, Alex's parents visited a Catholic priest. He was very sympathetic and said he himself had seen a ghost many years ago. He also told them that he thought he had some psychic powers. He promised he would visit the house in the evening and bless Alex's bedroom. The priest turned up and interviewed Alex in his bedroom for over an hour, taking notes throughout. After talking at length to the child, the priest came down to the living room and checked a few details he had taken down in his notebook. He sat facing Alex's parents and Kelly and asked them, "Is it true that there was a break-in about three months back?"

"Yes," said Alex's father, "but nothing was taken. They broke in through the back door. Why?"

"And the robbers took nothing. Don't you find that unusual?" inquired the priest, scratching his head. He looked at Alex's parents over his spectacles.

"What do you mean?" remarked Alex's mum.

"According to your son, the ghost, Jarvis, scared the robbers away from the house," said the priest.

Alex's parents looked at each other in disbelief, and the priest quoted the other notes from his little black book, "Er, let me see. Then there was a chip pan that went on fire, but a damp tea-towel mysteriously put the fire out, even though no one remembers who put the towel on the fire? Then you, madam," the priest addressed little Kelly, "were playing in the street with Alex and ran out in front of a car to get an ice cream and something lifted you off your feet and pulled you out the path of the car. Is that true?"

"Oh yeah, Mum. That's right. I forgot," said Kelly.

"And you, sir?" the priest addressed Alex's father. "You recently lost your car keys, and looked everywhere for them and then found them on the roof of your car. Is that true?"

"Yes. That was weird but what are you driving at?" asked Alex's Dad.

"All the work of one ghost named Jarvis. Your son says he's a friendly ghost who looks after you all like a guardian angel. I can't exorcise good ghosts, only evil spirits. You'd be better just turning a blind eye to him. He's done a lot of good." The priest then chuckled and, after drinking a cup of tea, left the house.

Unfortunately, only Alex and Kelly could accept poor Jarvis and so Alex's cowardly parents moved their family from the house. According to Alex, on the last night in their house, he heard Jarvis crying.

In 1994, a window cleaner was cleaning the windows of the same house and almost fell off his ladder when he saw a semi-transparent figure coming towards him. The window cleaner was not aware that the house was haunted and now gets his colleague to clean the windows of that house instead.

In 1997, a new family moved into the house and are apparently oblivious of the friendly ghost's activities. It will be interesting to see how long this unsuspecting family can remain ignorant of their ectoplasmic 'helper'.

The Vengeful Grave

In the summer of July 1997, a woman named Elaine visited a cemetery in Allerton, Liverpool, to put flowers on her mother's grave. Her mum had passed away ten years ago and her daughter visited the cemetery most Sundays to lay a bunch of flowers on the grave.

On this particular sunny afternoon, Elaine thought there was an unusual quietness in the cemetery. Hardly any traffic passed by on the main road outside. There were only three other people, all elderly, who were also visiting the graves of their loved ones.

Suddenly, a clod of earth whizzed past Elaine and landed with great force on the ground beside her. It had missed her head by inches. She looked around, expecting to see a mischievous child but there were no children to be seen. She had a little silent talk with her Mum and was about to walk away, when a pebble hit the stone urn on her mother's grave. Elaine had just filled the urn with flowers and she looked around in anger, determined to find the joker who was throwing things.

An elderly woman passed by and Elaine was about to ask her if she had seen any kids throwing things, when a small clod of earth came down and hit the old woman's leg. They looked at each other baffled. Elaine told the woman about the phantom stone-thrower and the pensioner called to her husband who was sitting in a parked car on the path. He came over and soon Elaine and the elderly couple were looking for the stone-throwers. Suddenly, a cluster of gravel pieces came down and showered the car on the path. The old man was furious and walked off down the grass verge that ran parallel to the row of gravestones. He then saw something that sent a shiver down his spine. A clod of earth lifted up off a grave and went hurtling into the air. The clod made a thud on a black marble headstone and sent soil flying everywhere. The old man ran back to his wife and Elaine and told them what he had seen.

The three of them walked over to the grave where the clod had seemingly taken off. The old woman said her husband had probably seen a mole but Elaine said she doubted that. Then the three of them looked on in disbelief as a handful of gravel and stones shot up from the grave and landed about twenty-five feet away on the same black marble stone. Some of the pieces of gravel and soil again landed on the car, which happened to be situated close to the marble headstone.

This strange phenomenon went on for about fifteen minutes but none of the observers would dare to venture close to the grave to get a better look at the spooky activity. Then, a middle-aged man approached with a bunch of flowers. He said that he was visiting his uncle's grave. He smiled when Elaine and the elderly couple recited their accounts of the stones shooting up off the grave. Without being told which grave was the origin of the strange stone-throwing activity, the man casually walked over to the weather-beaten white headstone and said, "This is the grave, isn't it?"

The three other people nodded, amazed at the way the man seemed unafraid of the eerie grave. Then the man told a bizarre story. He revealed, "This is the grave of a woman who lived in my neighbourhood. She was always fighting with her husband, always having a go at him over something or other. The police were forever being called out whenever she kicked off. Her husband was terrified of her because she tried to knife him once when they were having an argument. She used to throw plates and all sorts at him. When she died in a car crash, he was devastated. He told me he really loved her, even though they were always fighting."

The man then walked back towards the three spellbound onlookers. He pointed to the black marble grave that had been the target of the phantom missile-thrower and told them, "That's where her hen-pecked husband was buried. He died from cancer a couple of years ago. He was supposed to be buried in his wife's grave but his brother arranged for him to be buried there instead. You know what families are like!"

As the man explained all this, a pebble hit the black marble grave he was talking about. Elaine and the elderly couple jumped with fright but the man just laughed and turned to face the white marble headstone. He said, "Stop it, Margie. Rest in peace girl."

Within seconds the elderly couple were in their car. They let Elaine get in with them and the car screeched and sped off down the avenue outside the cemetery, leaving the brave man behind to tend to his uncle's grave.

Fatal Infatuation

A certain department store now covers the forgotten little cemetery of Church Alley, off Liverpool's Church Street. Thousands of shoppers stroll along this bustling thoroughfare quite unaware that, in their vicinity, the remains of Richard Worthington lie in the cold earth and have done so for one hundred and fifty years.

His ghost is said to have been seen in the department store that now stands on his unmarked grave. In 1977, a psychic who knew nothing of the story I am about to relate, was given permission to investigate the haunting of the department store. He said he felt that the spirit was heartbroken and that his surname was Worthing or Worthington. Perhaps when I tell you Worthington's story, his spirit will at last be able to rest in peace ...

In 1847, a nineteen year-old from Blackburn named Richard Worthington got a job at a wine merchant's cellar off Liverpool's Lime Street. At around six o'clock one October evening, Richard left the premises of his workplace and headed for his home near what is now Great Crosshall Street. As he strolled home, the heavens opened and torrential rain lashed down on him. Lightning flashed through the low, oppressive clouds and thunder rolled across the town.

As Richard ran blindly through the heavy rain, he collided with a girl at St George's Place, close to where St George's Hall stood. The impact sent the girl to the floor. Richard apologised to her repeatedly and picked her up. The girl was beautiful and spoke with a slight Welsh accent. She said her name was Megan Davies and that her life was in danger. The girl was absolutely saturated and her long, black, curly hair clung to her face, which was dripping wet. Her big, blue eyes stared timidly up at Richard, who was quite tall. Megan looked so vulnerable and it really was a case of love at first sight for the young man. He just gazed into those child-like eyes and he fell for her there and then. He took off his coat and wrapped it around the waif-like girl, then escorted her to the little rented house he had recently moved into. He sat Megan down in front of a blazing coal fire overstacked with wood, gave her a towel and then went up to his room to change into some dry clothes.

When Megan was dry, she told him a sad story. She had come to Liverpool from the Isle of Anglesey two years ago and had been living with a forty year-old man named Robert for over a year. She later discovered that he was married. After that huge shock, there came two more dreadful discoveries. The first was that he had another wife in the Everton district and, even more shockingly, he had murdered a third wife in Toxteth and had buried her somewhere in what are now the grounds of Sefton Park.

"How did you come upon all this information and why is your life in danger?" Richard asked, pouring her a glass of gin which she downed in one gulp. She trembled and told him that she had found Robert's diary in a chest in the attic and, when he found her reading the book, he chased her with a knife and tried to kill her. However, she escaped and had been on the run from him ever since. She pointed to a small scar on her left breast and said that was where the knife had grazed her during the cowardly attack.

"We must go to the police," Richard said angrily. He wondered how some brute could hurt a defenceless girl like Megan. His blood boiled at the thought.

Megan threw cold water on the idea about going to the law. "We can't Richard. Robert has friends in the police force and told me that he and the head of the Lancashire police are both freemasons in the same lodge. I fear it won't be long until the police arrest me and kill me on his orders. I'm ill with fear. I will have to flee Lancashire and return to Wales."

She started to cry and stood up, sobbing. "I am very grateful for the kind help you have shown but I must be on my way." Megan headed for the door but Richard would not let her leave, telling her that she should at least lay low in his lodgings for a week or so. He would tell no one she was staying there, so she would be safe from the evil bigamist and murderer.

Megan accepted Richard's offer and, the following day, she practically seduced the wine merchant's assistant as he was bathing in a tub by the fire. Richard had a strict puritanical upbringing and seemed uncomfortable with the girl at first but gradually became accustomed to sleeping with her each night. The neighbours in the street made much of the fact that the couple were 'living in sin' but he did not care. He was so in love with Meg and was secretly saving half of his apprentice wages each week to buy her an engagement ring. He had heard people talk about love but now he knew what it was all about; he was totally besotted with the girl from Anglesey.

In December of that year, Richard was making his way home to Meg with a bottle of fine wine and was astonished to see his beloved Meg battling with a tall grey haired man near the top of Dale Street. The man was shaking Megan by the shoulders and he had a long-bladed knife in his other hand. The ground was icy, and the stranger and Megan slid about as they grappled with each other. She was screaming at the man, who suddenly shouted, "You maniac! Trying to ruin my marriage!"

Richard ran across the icy cobblestones and shouted "Leave her alone!" The stranger let go of Megan and turned. Richard hit him on the head with the bottle of wine. The man fell onto his knees and Megan tried to grab the knife off him but the stranger held onto it and her fingers were cut by the blade. A crowd of bystanders then circled the three battling figures. Richard punched the man and tried to grab the knife from him but the man said, "Get away or I'll strike!"

Megan bit the hand that held the knife and the man screamed and slapped her face. This enraged Richard and he lunged forward and the stranger lifted his hand in defence. The blade of the knife went into Richard's chest. It pierced his heart and he fell down on the icy cobblestones, slowly dying as he reached out to Megan. But she ignored him as she pleaded with the stranger, "Robert! I'm sorry! Please don't desert me for her! I love you Robert! We can go away together!" Richard Worthington gave a puzzled look at the object of his love, then quietly died.

It later transpired that Megan was an escaped inmate from the Lunatic Asylum less than a hundred yards away, near Dawson Street. She had a history of inflicting wounds upon herself to get attention. The knife wound upon her breast that she had shown to the gullible Richard Worthington was one example. Megan also had psychotic tendencies and was often fixated by men she did not even know. After she had escaped from the asylum, she had followed a man around for months. She only knew his name was Robert and that he was married and lived in Toxteth. She would habitually sit on his doorstep, claiming he was her husband. When Robert threatened to call the police to remove her, she had tried to knife him and that had been the beautiful stalker's intention when she followed him to Dale Street on that fateful evening. Megan Davies was promptly locked away again in a more secure cell in the asylum and Richard Worthington, the teenager who had been blinded by her beauty, was laid to rest at the cemetery off Church Street.

The Green Eye of the Mersey

For thousands of years, the belief has persisted that certain people and objects can bring misfortune. In 1830, a British banker and gemstone collector named Henry Thomas Hope bought a large blue diamond which became known as the Hope Diamond. The origins of the oversized diamond are not known with any certainty but it is thought that the gem was cut from an even bigger diamond in the Golconda mines of India. There is a brief reference stating that the Hope Diamond was in the possession of King Louis XIV in the 18th century but that the stone was later lost during the French Revolution. Today, the Hope Diamond is kept at the Smithsonian Institute in America. However, the gemstone is regarded as a jinx, because every person who has owned it in the past either dropped dead of unnatural causes or committed suicide after buying the diamond.

Nearer to home is another example of an unlucky diamond, a spectacular emerald-like gemstone folklorists have nicknamed the 'Green Eye of the Mersey'.

On 21 October 1839, the night skies over Cheshire lit up with a blinding blue flash and scores of people saw a meteor fall to earth. The following morning, a farmer near Hollowmoor Heath discovered a small crater in his field. None of the cows would venture near the site of the meteoric impact and the farmer saw that there was a black object the size of a billiard ball embedded in the centre of the crater. The farmer showed the object to a clergyman and he passed it on to a friend William Ibbotson, who was an amateur astronomer. Ibbotson cleaned the meteorite and sawed it in half. In the middle of the globe there was an object that was so hard, the blade of the saw bounced off of it. Ibbotson cracked the meteorite open and saw that the object was a precious stone which was white, like an opal.

The unearthly gemstone was the size of an egg and had a peculiar flaw: the stone contained a circular emerald-coloured gemstone which made the stone resemble a glass eye with a green iris. Ibbotson sent a report of his find to the Royal Astronomical Society in London but never received a reply. He decided the 'Green Eye' as he called it, would be an unusual birthday gift for his niece who lived in Dublin. Five months later, Ibbotson boarded the steamer *William Huskisson* at Liverpool Docks but the ship never reached Ireland. It is not known why the steamship sank in the middle of the Irish Sea, since it was in excellent condition and its captain and crew had made the crossing hundreds of times. However, 40 passengers, including Mr Ibbotson, perished beneath the waves.

Weeks later, Ibbotson's suitcase was washed up on the coast of Hoylake and a man named George Peters opened the case and saw the strange Green Eye stone. After taking it to a jeweller who could not identify it, Peters decided to try and sell it in Liverpool. Twenty-four hours later, however, he died from a typhoid-like fever which claimed fifteen thousand victims in the town. So-called 'Fever Sheds' were opened at Mount Pleasant and the body of William Peters was literally thrown onto a heap of corpses in one of these sheds.

A poor Irishman named John Lorne stripped and searched the plague corpses and came across the Green Eye. He was naturally delighted at his lucky find and showed it to his friends at a pub in Hope Street, telling them he intended to get it valued. The landlord of the pub was very superstitious and thought the gemstone radiated evil. He told Lorne to take it off the premises. The Irishman laughed at the landlord's comments and went home.

Half an hour later, a boy ran into the pub and cried that Lorne was dying outside his lodging house in Percy Street. Lorne was impaled on the railings in front of the house and was barely alive. Two railings had gone through his back and were protruding from his chest. He coughed up blood as he gave an account of what had happened. He said a man had ran into his room and demanded the gemstone. There was a struggle, the man pushed Lorne through his open window and he had landed on the railings. Lorne's friends made the fatal mistake of trying to lift their companion off the railings, despite his terrible screams. Their well-meant intentions killed Lorne because as they lifted him, one railing severed a major artery and the other ruptured his liver.

The Green Eye gemstone fell out of Lorne's hand. One of the bystanders picked up the stone and a fight broke out over who should have it. The dead man's cousin, George Wishart, claimed it and he later emigrated to the Isle of Man. One day, Wishart decided to have the Green Eye mounted in a gold locket, but on his way to the jewellers, he dropped dead in the street. A pathologist said he had died from cardio-congestive failure but could not understand why, as Wishart had a cast-iron constitution.

Wishart's niece, a woman named May Allen, took possession of the jinxed gemstone and, within a year, five of her friends had died in tragic accidents. Even so, Mrs Allen refused to believe that the Green Eye was cursed.

In December 1909, she decided to visit relatives in Liverpool with her son Ernest. They both boarded a steamship named the *Ellan Vannin* and yes, you've guessed it, that ship sank in mysterious circumstances on its way to the port in Liverpool Bay. Look-outs in the Wirral lighthouse were horrified to see the *Ellan Vannin's* lights go out. Then, suddenly, the ship went under the waves within a couple of seconds. Everyone on board the ship was drowned and the cause of the sudden sinking has never been solved. The bodies of May and Ernest Allen were buried on the western side of St James's Cemetery, next to the Anglican Cathedral. Relatives of Mrs Allen said she had definitely taken the Green Eye stone with her to show it to her cousins in Liverpool, but the diamond was never found on her body. We must therefore presume that the cursed Green Eye gemstone is somewhere in the Mersey, probably within the wreck of the *Ellan Vannin* which still lies beneath the waves of Liverpool Bay. Considering the dark history of tragedy of all those who have owned it, perhaps the Green Eye of the Mersey should be left where it lies.

From a Window

In the month of May, 1866, Liverpool was hit by a cholera epidemic which killed hundreds. One of these unfortunate victims was Maureen Allen, a beautiful ravenhaired girl who was only sixteen and the youngest member of an Irish family that had recently settled in Rose Place in Everton.

Maureen was laid in a coffin and the Irish custom of observing a wake commenced. The authorities were opposed to this as they did not like the idea of a body that had died of cholera being put into an open coffin. However, the Allen family told them to mind their own business. The wake went ahead, as did the ritual drinking, feasting and lamentation. On the evening of the wake at around seven o'clock, every member of the Allen family headed for a pub in Great Homer Street to drown their sorrows. George's nineteen year-old niece Shannon, who had only been in Liverpool for a week, volunteered to look after the house.

At eight o'clock that night, Richard O'Hare, an old friend of George Allen, the father of the deceased girl, knocked on the front door of the Allen's family home. O'Hare wasn't aware that Maureen had died as he had not seen the girl since she was a toddler. O'Hare knocked again and there was no answer. As he was about to turn away, one of the bedroom windows of the house opened with a grating sound. A girl looked out and smiled.

"Do the Allens live here, sweetheart?" O'Hare asked the girl.

"Yes, they've all gone down the pub," said the girl.

O'Hare asked which pub and the girl told him it was on the corner of Great Homer Street.

"Thank you, sweetheart," he replied and started to whistle as he made his way to the pub. When he got there, he said to George, "Hello there, and how is life treating you?" George Allen tearfully told his friend that he had just lost his daughter. O'Hare said that he was extremely sorry and hugged his friend and his wife.

When the Allens returned to the house they could get no answer. George shouted through the letterbox, "Shannon, open the door girl," but Shannon did not reply. "That girl has been more of a hindrance than a help since she came over," George told his friend as he delved into his pockets looking for the keys.

"Shannon will be the girl I talked to this evening. She's a real beauty, George. Her hair was blacker than yours and her voice was like silk," said O'Hare, staggering behind his friend.

"No," said George, "Shannon's a redhead. You must have called at the wrong house earlier."

"I called here, George, and a girl with long black hair came to that window up there," said O'Hare, pointing up to the open window with a solemn look.

Shannon suddenly came down the road, arm in arm with a local boy. When she saw her angry uncle, his family and Mr O'Hare, she told the boy to leave. The boy kissed her and hurried away in the other direction.

"Where the hell have you just been? You're supposed to be minding the house!" George Allen roared at her.

"I only went to the corner to post a letter to my father. That's all, Uncle George," said Shannon, unaware that she had a lovebite on her neck plain for all to see.

"This actress here is Shannon," George told his friend O'Hare.

"George, that wasn't the girl who spoke to me at the window," O'Hare whispered. But Mrs Allen and her three sons overheard him and they drew nearer out of curiosity.

"Are you sure Richard?" asked Mr Allen, perplexed.

O'Hare said, "As true as God is in Heaven, George. May I never draw another breath, but the girl who spoke to me from that window had black hair. She looked nothing like your niece here."

"You must have been at the wrong house. You must have been talking to Billy Jones's daughter next door, you old reprobate." George reasoned with himself and nodded to Shannon to open the door with the keys he had entrusted her with.

When O'Hare went up to the room where the girl had talked to him from the window, he almost fainted. The girl he had been talking to was lying dead in her coffin. She was Maureen Allen. George and his sons pounced upon O'Hare when he said he had talked to Maureen, attacking him out of fear rather than rage.

"Throw him out," George commanded and his three sons lifted O'Hare up by his armpits when Mrs O'Hare said, "Wait!" The boys stopped immediately and looked at their mother.

Mrs Allen said: "Richard O'Hare has done some things in his past but he has never been a liar. Now look, the window's open and so are the curtains. I distinctly remember drawing those curtains as it is the custom to do so in a wake and that window was shut. And secondly, Richard didn't know Maureen was at rest in this room but he said this was the room she spoke to him from. Finally, he described Maureen to a tee and we all know Billy Jones's fat daughter is nothing like Maureen."

"What are you getting at, Maggie?" George asked his wife edgily.

"Someone opened the curtains and window in this room," said Mrs Allen as she glanced at Shannon, who was standing in the doorway.

"I didn't, Aunt Maggie. Before the Seven Sacraments, I can't even come into this room where our Maureen is. It distresses me to see her lying there." said Shannon.

"Who opened the window and curtains then?" asked Mr Allen once again.

"I told you, George," said Richard O'Hare. "Before All Mighty God, it was Maureen."

And, as Richard finished the sentence, a strange icy draught passed through the room and the curtains fluttered ...

Victim of Gossip

The following story, which took place in Liverpool in the seventeenth century, is a tale about the dangers of jumping to conclusions.

In the year 1627, a farmer named Jeremiah Malins was ploughing his field, near to what is now Huyton. Farmer Malins noticed, out of the corner of his eye, a woman running through the woodland which bordered the field. The farmer watched as the woman disappeared into the woods and observed that she had left a bundle of some sort at the base of a tree. He left his plough and went to see what the bundle was. It was a newly-born baby girl swathed in old rags. The farmer, who was a widower, decided to adopt her and named her Anna after his late wife.

Anna grew into a young woman of breathtaking beauty and every man she met was enchanted and infatuated with her. Anna could not understand her popularity and why, almost every day, some love-struck man proposed to her. There was no mirror in the farmhouse and she was not aware of her beauty.

One chilly Christmas Eve afternoon in 1647, Anna, who had now turned twenty, left the farmhouse to gather wood for the fire, but never returned. Farmer Malins expressed his concern about Anna's safety to a neighbouring farmer and two woodsmen but they assured him that Anna was probably seeing a secret boyfriend and would soon return.

By midnight, there was still no sign of the girl, so Farmer Malins lit a torch and went into the woods. He found a piece of Anna's torn dress and picked it up. He shouted the girl's name and scoured the woods and the countryside until the sun came up. Anna was still nowhere to be found.

Three days later, the gossipers of rural Liverpool started rumours that Jeremiah Malins had raped his adopted daughter and killed her after making her pregnant. These cruel whisperings spread like wildfire through the community and finally reached the ears of a Colonel Birch, a power-mad military commander stationed at the Tower of Liverpool. Birch and his soldiers visited Malins at his farm and accused the farmer of rape and murder. Malins protested and was so outraged that he punched Birch in the face. To make matters worse, Birch found the piece of Anna's skirt on the table with buttons on it. Furthermore, an old woman called Mrs Todd came forward and said she had seen the farmer kissing and molesting the girl in the woods by the light of the moon on Christmas Eve.

Colonel Birch had heard enough and decided to force the farmer to confess. He chained him to the underside of a hay-cart which was pulled by horses for two miles. At the end of the journey, Malins was unchained and Birch saw that the farmer's back had been badly scraped and was dripping with blood. Malins still would not confess to killing Anna so Birch transported him to the Tower of Liverpool in Water Street.

Malins was stripped naked and put on the rack where he was slowly stretched until his shoulder was pulled out of its socket and his ankle ligaments snapped. The farmer yelled out in agony, shouting, "Please have mercy!" Birch was a renowned sadist and stood there drinking wine and sighing with pleasure. The farmer was removed from the rack and tied to a chair. His hands were bound to the arms of the chair and a masked man entered the chamber with a hammer. He put long, three inch tacks under the nails of Malins' fingers and tapped them in with the hammer. Malins screamed out for the man to stop but the torturer struck his kneecap with the hammer.

"You killed Anna, didn't you?" demanded the drunken Colonel Birch and he gave the farmer an ultimatum. "Say you did and you'll be tortured no more."

"I didn't kill her, by almighty God, I swear I didn't," groaned Farmer Malins, with blood trickling from his fingers.

The records of what happened next are unclear and unreliable but one version of events is that something unparalleled in the history of torture took place: Jeremiah Malins was squashed between two panels of wood which were nailed together, so that the farmer could hardly breathe. Then, the two chief carpenters of the Tower were ordered to saw down the length of the sandwiched panels with a long woodcutter's saw. When the blade was inches from the farmer's skull, he allegedly confessed that he had killed Anna but Colonel Birch told the carpenters to continue and despite the horrific screams, they sawed downwards through the farmer's head, cutting it into half. Birch told them to keep on sawing until they had cut the body through. A mob outside the Tower cheered when they heard the news of the farmer's execution and demanded to see the bisected body, which was later put on display.

Then, on New Years Day 1648, the missing girl Anna returned in the best of health at the farmstead. The shocked community listened to her account of where she had been since that fateful Christmas Eve. Anna said that she had been travelling with a band of gypsy folk she had met in the woods. They had taken her to a fair in Chester on Christmas Eve and exhibited her in a sideshow as a direct descendant of Cleopatra.

When Anna was told that Farmer Malins had been tried with her murder and executed, she fainted. Colonel Birch sent a messenger to Anna with an apology and then arrested old Mrs Todd, the woman who said she had seen the farmer molesting his daughter. Mrs Todd was taken to the Tower and a trainee executioner, a young boy of fifteen, was allowed to practice his beheading technique on the old woman. She was carried to the chopping block, trembling with fear. Two soldiers positioned the old woman's head over the chopping block. The young boy hit her neck with the axe and her head flew across the room. The head still seemed alive. As it fell on the floor of the chamber, the tongue squirmed outside of the mouth. Colonel Birch picked up the head and exclaimed, "See how the gossiper's tongue still flaps, even in death!"

Resurrection Mary

In the autumn of 1995, a Wavertree couple moved into a beautiful old Victorian house near Druids Cross Gardens in the Calderstones area of south Liverpool. In the daytime, the house and garden seemed picturesque and quiet but when darkness fell, the atmosphere changed. A series of supernatural occurrences sent the couple in search of a ghost researcher. The couple said that on most nights after ten o'clock, they heard the chilling sound of something being dragged up the gravel path outside.

Whenever this sound was heard, the couple's dog Arthur would become hysterical and run upstairs in a terrible state. The couple's cat Jinjee, on the other hand, always went to the window and stared out into the darkness with a fascinated look, as if she could see something. Jinjee was much braver than her owners because the couple never dared to look outside when they heard the eerie dragging sound. They just sat inside and held onto each other as they heard the 'thing' outside crawl up to the doorstep and rap on the door for a while.

When the ghost researcher arrived, he taped the sounds and, on one occasion, he actually caught a glimpse of a hazy, white object on the gravel path and tried to photograph it. However, nothing appeared when the picture was developed. One night, when the dragging sound was heard, the ghost researcher went outside and saw pieces of gravel being dragged along with the invisible object. He researched the history of the house in Calderstones, determined to find out if anything unusual had happened there in the past. The ghostbuster passed the address to a circle of local historians and one of them found a piece of information that threw light on the strange haunting.

In 1750, on the site of the couple's Calderstones home, a doctor named Charles Johnson had an affair with a young girl named Mary Jenkins. Mary was only eighteen but was exceptionally beautiful with long blonde hair, big blue eyes and pale, delicate skin. She was uneducated and worked as a maid for the doctor who, finding her irresistible, had an affair with her resulting in her becoming pregnant.

Doctor Johnson's wife died soon after the pregnancy became known and young Mary said that they could now be married and tell the world about their love. However, the doctor wanted to marry a wealthy woman named Georgina Clayton, who had recently inherited her late father's estate.

Mary Jenkins pleaded with Doctor Johnson and she got down on her knee and kept saying, "Please say you will marry me. I'm having your child." Johnson would have none of it, threw a tantrum and hit her across the face. Mary sobbed, "I'll tell everyone about our love and our baby." Infuriated, Johnson reached for the poker near the fireplace and struck his young lover on the head.

An old widow named Hannah Cleveland heard the screams and went to Johnson's cottage and peeped through the window. She saw him bending over Mary Jenkins, who looked lifeless, and the tearful doctor was saying, "Mary my love … what have I done? Please open your eyes."

The Widow Cleveland went to the local vicar and told him of the dreadful deed. He and a mob of locals turned up at the cottage but there was no sign of young Mary. The poker was examined but had evidently been cleaned and had no blood on it. Doctor Johnson denied the attack had taken place and said he had not set eyes upon the maid for over two days. He said she often went missing and was believed to be staying with a lover. Johnson said the Mrs Cleveland was mentally unbalanced and prone to hallucinating since the death of her husband, but the widow insisted that her story was true. The vicar said that as there was no evidence of any murder, he could do nothing. But tongues in the community started wagging as the weeks passed and Mary Jenkins did not appear. Many believed that the Widow Cleveland had been telling the truth and that Johnson had disposed of Mary's body.

When Georgina Clayton, the woman Johnson was to marry, heard about Mary's strange disappearance, she asked him if he had killed her. Johnson became enraged and said, "I swear before almighty God! I only wish Mary Jenkins would return so she could prove my innocence! Please believe me, I have nothing to do with Mary Jenkins's disappearance."

"Oh, I'm sorry I doubted you, Charles," Georgina comforted her fiancé.

A week later, the couple married and enjoyed a short honeymoon in Scotland. When they returned, nobody would talk to them and the gossipers openly pointed Johnson out when he passed by in the street.

"They still maintain that you have something to do with the maid's disappearance," said Georgina, one stormy night at the cottage.

Johnson turned out all the lights and lit a candle. He took Georgina by the hand and led her up to the bedroom saying, "I've told you my dear, by the heavens above us, I wish Mary Jenkins would return to prove my innocence."

At that precise moment, the couple heard a noise outside the cottage. Doctor Johnson went to the bedroom window and opened it. Down in the garden was a horrible sight. In the moonlight, the half-decomposed body of Mary Jenkins was dragging itself along the path towards the house on its stomach. Johnson stared down at the ghoulish figure which looked up at him, reaching out with a bony skeletal hand. Her eyes were set in large circular black sockets and the girl's cheeks had collapsed inwards. Her mouth opened and a faint voice said, "Charles, I love you".

Johnson slammed the window and drew the curtains. Georgina asked him what he had witnessed and he started to tremble. His hand shook so badly that he had to put the candlestick down. He ran to bed and hid under the bedclothes like a frightened child.

"What's the matter, Charles?" Georgina cried, as she flung back the curtains and looked out the window.

"No!!" shouted the doctor from his bed. "Don't look out!"

But Georgina did and she recoiled in horror at the sight of the rotting corpse, which had now dragged itself along the path to the front doorstep. It's bony fingers rapped and scratched on the door. Georgina was suspicious about the identity of the crawling corpse and she turned and looked at her new husband.

"That is Mary Jenkins, is it not?"

He begged her to come away from the window but Georgina started to scream at the idea of being in the same room as a murderer and also at the sight of the animated corpse. She ran screaming downstairs and left by the back door. She told the vicar and a local magistrate and they headed to Johnson's cottage with a mob who were hungry for justice. However, they were cheated because Johnson was found sitting up in bed with a look of terror on his face. He was dead and his bulging eyes were fixed on something. They stared in horror at the floor beside the bed but there was nothing there nor was there any corpse on the path outside. A subsequent search of the garden revealed the shallow grave of the missing and badly decomposed Mary Jenkins and her unborn child.

For many years, the Johnson cottage remained empty because people who lived there often reported hearing the sound of 'Resurrection Mary' dragging herself from her grave in the garden. The couple who recently moved into the house in Calderstones were naturally horrified at the ghost researcher's chilling discovery ...

A Surprise Appearance at the Cavern Club

The following story is a particularly strange one. It concerns three men who used to visit the Cavern Club in Mathew Street, way back in the days before Merseybeat, when the Cavern was a jazz club. The story is told all over Liverpool and has been in circulation since the early 1960s. Nobody knows whether there is any truth behind the tale or if it is just a so-called 'urban myth'. Strangely enough, in every version of the story, the names of the characters are always the same. Furthermore, according to an article in the *Liverpool Echo* in the late 1950s, the manager of the Cavern claimed that there was a ghost that haunted the ladies' toilets ...

Around 1957, a man named Alan Sytner opened the Cavern Club in Liverpool to provide a venue for the then thriving jazz scene. As most people know, the Cavern was basically a collection of arched warehouse cellars in the heart of downtown Liverpool where the Beatles first came to prominence.

In the late 1950s, three men went to the club one evening with their girlfriends and had a great time listening to the jazz bands. The men were Johnny, Tony and Peter and, at four in the morning, when most of the clubgoers had gone home, the three men and their girlfriends sat at a table, smoking and chatting away. The conversation turned from sport, to politics, to religion, to the meaning of life and finally resulted in an argument about the occult.

At this point, one of the men's girlfriends, a girl named Rita, said that one of the toilets in the Cavern was supposed to be haunted, but Peter, who was a hard-boiled sceptic, said the ghost story was probably just a publicity gimmick invented by the Cavern's owner. One of the members of management overheard Peter's remark and insisted that there really was a ghost. He said that one of the bouncers had recently seen the ghost, a man dressed in black.

At this point, Johnny suggested that everyone present should gather round the table and join hands to summon the ghost up, claiming that he knew the actual words to evoke a spirit. The girlfriends thought it would be exciting and urged their boyfriends and the bouncers to join in. Everyone thought it was a joke except a young man named Tony, who was not exactly religious but said the occult should not be regarded in such a light-hearted manner. He sat at another table, lit up a cigarette and watched the proceedings nervously.

With everyone but Tony gathered around the table, Johnny said, "Right, turn the lights off. Get a candle or something."

A candle could not be found but someone brought a small electric torch to the circle, switched it on, and then placed it in the centre of the table. The lights were switched off and all the people around the table joined hands.

There was a scream. One of the bouncers had put his hand up one of the girl's dresses for a laugh. Johnny said, "Stop messing about. We need absolute silence."

There were a few sniggers but then a strange silence descended into the cellars. After a minute, Johnny called out, "O Lord of darkness, I invite you into the Cavern. Give us a sign so we may believe."

One of the girls said, "And get a move on 'cos I wanna go to the toilet."

A shadow walked across the darkened room. It was a tall man wearing a black suit and a black polo-neck sweater, hardly in fashion at the time. His black fringe was combed back into the style of the so-called 'DA cut' popularised by the film star Tony Curtis. All the girls looked at him but none of them were scared. They thought the stranger was just a clubgoer who had been part of the stay-behind. All the girls later said that the man was very attractive and had magnetic dark eyes.

Tony, who was seated at the other table on his own, thought the man was evil from the moment he set eyes upon him and noticed that the stranger seemed to come from the direction of the toilets.

"I am Lucifer," said the man, in a rich deep voice. He then smirked and studied the shocked expressions of the people at the table.

"Stop messing about,"said Johnny, "we're trying to hold a seance here."

"You idiot," replied the stranger, "I am Lucifer. You didn't expect me to have horns, did you?"

"Oh, you're the Devil, like?" sneered one of the bouncers trying to impress the girls.

The stranger nodded, "I haven't got hoofed feet either."

"Johnny, I'm scared. Turn the lights on," cried Rita, shaking hysterically.

"Relax, dear," said the stranger, "I'm not as bad as I'm painted."

The sceptical Peter retorted, "There's no such thing as the Devil."

"If you believe in God, you must believe in me too," said the man in black, "unless you are an atheist, of course."

"Yes I am, actually" Peter responded in a matter-of-fact way.

"Then if you don't believe in me, can I have your soul?" asked the stranger.

Peter laughed nervously, "But I don't believe ..."

"Give me your soul then!" shouted the stranger.

"Give him your soul, mate!" joked the bouncer and chuckled, "Soulmate, gerrit?" But no one was laughing. The atmosphere was tense with a mounting sense of terror.

"Okay, take it then." Peter grinned but he seemed to be very uneasy.

"No! Don't, Peter! Don't!" shouted Tony from the other table. He stood up but was afraid to come over.

"Thank you," said the stranger reaching out in the direction of Peter with his hand and clutching at something in the air.

The torch started to fade. Within seconds it was just a dim orange filament, then the Cavern was in complete blackness.

"That was one amateurish set-up," said one of the bouncers, almost falling over the table in the dark. He went to switch on the lights but they did not go on. "Oh, don't tell me the fuses have gone again," said the bouncer groping in the darkness.

During this time, a voice whispered in Tony's ear, "I'll be back for you one day and your god won't be able to save you."

Tony cried, "In the name of our saviour Jesus Christ I tell you to leave."

Suddenly the lights came on and everyone rose from the table. All but Peter who slumped forwards, hitting his face on the table-top. He seemed drunk but, when his mates took him home to his flat in Smithdown Lane, he did not seem to be breathing. He was taken by a taxi to the Royal Hospital in Pembroke Place and was certified dead on arrival. The coroner who performed the post-mortem examination later said that Peter, who was twenty-seven, had the body of an eighteen year-old and seemed to have been in perfect health. A verdict of death by natural causes was recorded but all the people who attended the frightening seance believed that Peter had died because he had foolishly given permission to the Devil to wrench his soul from his body.

Bad Moon on the Rise

As most people will probably know, a werewolf is a person who changes into a wolf-like creature when the moon is full. This is a myth, as most country-dwellers who know their folklore will tell you. The werewolf is described as a large, unidentified species of wolf which has no tail and is usually quite long, often over seven feet in length. The animal carries out most of its hunting at night when the moon is full, yet these strange creatures also prowl most nights regardless of whether the moon is full or not. Most of us have heard of the Beast of Bodmin Moor and the Surrey Puma; strange unidentified animals which have been tearing hundreds of sheep and cattle apart for years but there is also a violent creature nearer to our own neck of the woods which has also killed people. This animal is known as the Welsh Werewolf.

Records of an enormous wolf-like animal in North Wales date back to 1790, when a stagecoach travelling between Denbigh and Wrexham was allegedly attacked and overturned by an enormous black beast almost as long as the coach horses. The beast tore into one of the horses and killed it, while the other horse broke free from its harness and galloped off into the night whinnying in terror.

The attack took place just after dusk, with a full moon on the horizon. The moon that month seemed blood red, probably because of dust in the stratosphere from a recent forest fire in the Hatchmere area. The locals in North Wales and Cheshire thought the moon's colour was a sign that something evil was at large and the superstitious phrase, "Bad moon on the rise" was whispered in travellers' inns across the region.

In the winter of 1791, a farmer went into his snow-covered field just seven miles east of Gresford and saw enormous tracks that looked like those of an overgrown wolf. He followed the tracks with a blacksmith for two miles and they led into a farmstead where every single animal had either been torn to shreds or mortally wounded. One snow-covered field was just a lake of blood, dotted with carcasses of sheep, cattle and even the farmer's dog. The farmer was found locked up in his house in a terrible state. He was physically unharmed but terrified, having barricaded himself in after witnessing an enormous black animal that resembled a wolf ripping the throat out of his dog. The animal had then turned on the farmer but he had just managed to escape to the farmhouse in time. He had bolted the heavy oak door and hidden under a table in the kitchen, armed only with a pitchfork. The wolf had pounded on the heavy oak door, almost knocking it off its hinges, before standing up on its hind legs like a human and looking in through the windows of the farmhouse. The beast foamed at the mouth as it peered in, then bolted from the window to commit wholesale carnage on the farm.

Each of the sheep were left as pelts of wool with a head attached, lying flat on the snow like a woollen mat. The beast had even eaten sections of the animal's spines and no one had ever seen a predator do anything like that before. The church set up patrols in search of what was suspected to be an evil werewolf and bands of villagers braved the freezing blizzards with lanterns, muskets and pitchforks in search of the ravenous beast, but only its tracks were ever seen.

Seven years later, two men walking across the Bickerton Hills in Cheshire saw something that sent them running for their lives. The full moon had just risen and as it peeped over the hilltop, the travellers saw the silhouette of an enormous unidentified animal against the lunar disk. The animal lifted its head and let out a bloodcurdling howl which echoed through the Cheshire hills. The two men rushed into an inn and refused to continue their journey until morning. At dawn on the following day, the mutilated bodies of two vagrants were found in a wood just five miles from the inn. It did not seem to be murder because their bodies had been slashed to ribbons by something which had claws like knives. One of the victims had tried to cross a stream as he fled the scene and had been pounced upon in the waters. His head had been torn off and was never found. The head of the other victim was found stripped of its face and ears in another part of the wood. The jaws of the animal that killed the man must have been extremely powerful because the victim's skull had been cracked and splintered during the gruesome attack.

Someone wrote an anonymous letter and posted it to the local minister. The letter claimed the beast that had killed the men had been a werewolf which had been on the loose in that area of Cheshire and Wales for over a hundred years. It also said that the attack had happened during an eclipse of the moon, when the moon passes into the earth's shadow and turns dark red. He claimed that he had heard the terrible screams of the tramps who were slaughtered by the animal. The writer told the minister to paint crosses on the doors of each dwelling in the village because the werewolf was driven in its bloodlust by the evil spirit of a Welsh warlock, who had been burnt to the stake by the ancestors of the villagers in the year 1400.

The attacks by the large black wolf gradually died out and the people of Cheshire and Wales breathed a sigh of relief but two centuries later, attacks have been reported again.

In February 1992, a Welsh newspaper called the *Western Mail* reported sightings of a strange bear-like animal that had been seen across Wales. In the north of the country, a farmer who had spotted the animal on the night of a full moon found two of his fully grown seventy pound lambs ripped apart. One of the lambs was flattened as if it had been run over by a farm tractor. There were around seventy further sightings between 1992 and 1994 and London Zoo gave the farmers in the area advice for trapping the unknown predator.

Cages baited with steaks and equipped with special trap-doors were installed on the farms in the hope that the beast would venture into one of them. The animal did go into one cage but when the door sprung shut, it pulled two steel bars open and escaped. London Zoo said some lunatic must have helped the animal escape but the farmer said that the animal had pulled the bars apart itself. London Zoo experts said no known animal could have done something like that, even a grisly bear.

One explanation was that a wolverine was on the loose, but the tracks left by the violent animal seem to indicate that it was a large variety of wolf. An American expert on animal tracks said the prints left by the animal strongly resembled fossilised tracks left by the long extinct sabre-toothed tiger. However, the sabre-toothed tiger has not roamed Britain since the Pleistocene Era over two million years ago. From the pattern of sightings made after 1995, it seems that the so-called 'Welsh Werewolf' is steadily moving eastwards towards Cheshire and Merseyside ...

Evil Assailant

The following chilling story is from the annals of the now-defunct Lancashire Spiritualists Society which was based in West Derby, Liverpool at the turn of the century.

There is a Victorian house in Bidston on the Wirral, which was once the scene of a disturbing supernatural incident that allegedly occurred in 1920. The house was bought by two sisters, Victoria and Margaret Webster, who had been left a substantial legacy in 1919. Margaret was nineteen and Victoria was twenty-four. They originally came from Neston but moved to the beautiful terraced house in Bidston after the death of their father, a wealthy shipping magnate who left his daughters thousands of pounds. Mrs Webster died after giving birth to Margaret in 1901.

The Webster sisters soon settled into their new home and found the neighbours quite agreeable. Both sisters were said to be very attractive and caught the attention of many men in their new neighbourhood.

One night early in December 1920, Victoria went into town with a local government clerk named William. She had been seeing him for three months and he was very much in love with her. Victoria's teenage sister Margaret stayed at home and read a book. Around midnight, Victoria still hadn't returned so Margaret went to bed, where she read her book by the light of a candle. She started to doze, when she thought she heard a noise downstairs. Margaret got up and went to the landing, then shouted down the stairs, "Is that you Victoria?"

No reply came, but Margaret saw the shadow of a figure flit across the bottom flight of steps and heard a faint chuckle. Margaret thought it was William teasing her sister. Margaret liked William; he made her laugh with his foolish games, so she went downstairs, carrying the candle, expecting to see William staging some prank.

Margaret reached the bottom flight of steps and saw the flickering flames of the coal fire still burning in the grate. Margaret had forgotten to put the safety guard around the fire and as she walked to the parlour, she noticed a figure standing in the shadows of the hall to her left. She turned, and saw a strange-looking man standing there. He wore a long curly white wig like the one worn by a judge and a long embroidered satin coat with large turned-up sleeves, just like the coats worn in the eighteenth century. Beneath this, the stranger wore a silvery waistcoat and instead of trousers, he had on outdated breeches to his knees. On the lower parts of his legs, the man wore white stockings and on his feet wore square-toed shoes with shiny buckles. What really scared young Margaret was the intruder's face, which was thickly covered in white make-up. He looked at the terrified girl with an evil expression, then rushed towards her.

Margaret dropped the candlestick and ran into the parlour. She closed the door behind her and leaned against it with her heart pounding. The intruder started to steadily force the door open, finally charging at it, throwing Margaret across the room with the impact. The stranger started to chase the terrified teenager around the table and, because she was so traumatised, she found herself unable to scream. Her throat seemed weak with terror. The man suddenly stopped chasing and, in a weird accent, said "Now my pretty one, stay still, for I must have you." With that, he jumped onto the table with amazing agility and leapt onto the girl.

She fell to the floor by the fire and he started to molest her. He tore at her dress and violently kissed and bit at her neck and breasts. The girl felt powerless until she saw the hot poker in the grate. She grabbed it with her left hand and pushed it into the attacker's face. He let out a scream and clawed Margaret's face. The girl retaliated by clubbing him on the head with the poker.

Margaret suddenly regained the power to shout out and she let out a scream that sent her weird attacker running from the room. Margaret got to her feet and heard his footsteps running down the stairs to the cellar. The girl ran into the street in a dreadful state and Victoria and William came running to her aid. Several neighbours also came out to see what all the screams were about. Margaret screamed that the assailant had run into the cellar but when William went down to look, he found the cellar empty.

William and Victoria thought the tale of the eighteenth century attacker was a bit far-fetched and virtually accused Margaret of having an over-active imagination. However, Victoria was unable to account for the 'love-bites' on Margaret's neck and chest and the scratch-marks on her face. She guessed that Margaret had been canoodling with some local boy who had fled when he heard her older sister coming home.

Margaret stuck by her story and weeks later, Victoria and William also saw the out-dated man in the powdered wig peering out of the parlour window one Sunday morning when they were returning from church.

The Webster girls learnt from their neighbours that the previous owners had left, believing that the house was haunted. They said that in the wee small hours, the sinister apparition of an old-fashioned-looking man often appeared in the bedroom of their daughter with a lecherous look in his eye.

In the winter of 1922, a water pipe burst in the Webster sisters' house and workmen were called in. While the workmen were digging to get to the pipe, which ran under the cellar, they unearthed an unmarked red mahogany coffin. When this coffin was opened by the authorities, it revealed the skeleton of a man wearing a long white curly wig and tattered early eighteenth century clothes. The clothes and the wig matched the same wig and clothes as those worn by the sinister intruder who had recently attacked Margaret Webster.

Local historians later deduced that the skeleton was that of Richard Tilly, a notorious but wealthy eighteenth century rake and Satan worshipper. Tilly was charged with sorcery, sacrilege, blackmail, rape and even a ritual murder but had bribed the magistrate and escaped sentencing by promising to live in obscurity. It is thought that the satanist was secretly buried on the site of the Webster sisters' house around the year 1730. In Tilly's coffin there was a crumbling book entitled *Lucifer's Bible* and, on the front page, there was the sign of an upside down pentagram, the symbol of a Satanist. The text was too faded to read but probably contained references to satanism and black magic practices.

Understandably, the Webster sisters soon left the house and moved to North Wales. Tilly's coffin was not allowed to be buried in a Christian churchyard and is thought to have been re-buried near Bidston Hill.

When the Devil Walked through Liverpool

On 12 January 1866, a great snow storm struck Liverpool. The blizzard was so fierce that it blew down telegraph lines and all communication with London and the rest of the country was suspended for over a week. As temperatures plunged below zero, the River Mersey froze over and Liverpool gradually came to a standstill. People hurried indoors to escape the big freeze. Liverpool soon resembled a ghost town; not a soul roamed the snow-covered streets.

At six o'clock the following morning, a policeman in the south-end of the city came upon a curious sight. In the fresh virgin snow on Great George Street, he noticed a trail of what seemed to be animal tracks. At first sight, the tracks looked like hoof prints but they were very peculiar. It was as if the animal had put one hoof exactly in front of the other and walked in a precise straight line. The policeman measured the distance between each horseshoe-shaped print and saw that it was eight inches. He knew of no animal that could walk in such a manner.

He followed the trail and saw that the tracks could not have been made by any four-legged animal he was aware of. Nothing impeded the progress of the unidentified animal; the tracks went right up Great George Street and were found on each side of a factory wall. Stranger still, at one point, the tracks went across the roof of a snow-covered house in Oldham Street, where a postman had also noticed the strange prints. The trail extended up St Anne Street and Scotland Road where they suddenly came to a dead end, as if the strange creature had taken off like a bird at that point.

News of the eerie trail spread across Liverpool and the local population, which comprised of many superstitious Irish immigrants, thought there was something unearthly about the prints in the snow. People were soon referring to the tracks as the Devil's footprints, believing that Satan had strolled through the deserted streets of Liverpool. Who else had hoofed feet? And who else could walk over walls and rooftops? Others thought the culprit was Spring-Heeled Jack, a legendary figure who could make tremendous leaps into the air. Other people blamed otters, rats, a three-legged horse and someone suggested that perhaps the trail had been made by a rope dangling from a balloon but none of the theories fitted the facts.

The mystery deepened when several people, including a postmaster in Richmond Row, Everton, claimed that they had heard strange pipe music at around four o'clock on the morning that the tracks were made. This convinced people that it was the Devil who has always been depicted as playing pipes like the Greek god of mischief, Pan.

After the thaw, the footprints incident soon faded from the public's memory. However not many people in Liverpool knew that similar footprints had been seen eleven years before in Devon, again after a snowstorm. Also, in the reign of King Richard I, at York, a monk wrote about hoof-like tracks which appeared on the ground after a fierce lightning storm.

So, what made the tracks on that winter's morning in Liverpool? Was it just some wild animal like a badger that had ventured into a seemingly deserted town? Or did the Devil really once walk through Liverpool?

The Homesick Passenger

In 1993, a Liverpool cab driver named Alan bought a second-hand hackney cab from Brian, another taxi driver who lived in his street. The taxi seemed alright but when Alan was on night duty, the vehicle started acting very peculiarly. He was driving up Townsend Lane, near Cabbage Hall, to collect a woman in Cherry Lane, when the cab started slowing down. Suddenly, the steering wheel twisted itself left in the cabbie's hands and the cab turned down a street. Alan regained control of the vehicle and narrowly missed hitting a skip full of rubbish at the side of the road. He stopped the vehicle and put the handbrake on. He turned the wheel to check the steering but it seemed okay and Alan started wondering if his tired mind was playing tricks on him. He put the incident down to an involuntary spasm in his left arm and drove on.

The place where the cab had stopped was Chapel Road and, at the end of the road, Alan turned the wheel right to turn into Manningham Road. Upon reaching a junction, the wheel turned left of its own accord again and this time he wrestled with the wheel to bring it back but the taxi-cab turned into Pinehurst Road, where he stalled it. He got on the phone to Brian, the man he had bought the cab from, even though it was after midnight, Alan gave him a right earful although Brian insisted that there was nothing wrong with the steering. When Alan told him where the incident had happened, Brian became silent.

"Did you say Pinehurst Road?" Brian asked.

"Yeah, that's right. Look, I'm coming round to your's now, if I can get there in this write-off."

Alan was a rather stocky man who didn't suffer fools gladly and when he turned up at Brian's flat, he was very angry. Brian invited him in and convinced him that there was nothing wrong with the cab. After all, it had just had its MOT and was in pristine condition mechanically. Brian made Alan a strong coffee and calmed him down. Half an hour later, he was on the road again looking for fares and the remainder of the morning was trouble-free.

Over the next few weeks, Alan learned that the trouble with the steering only seemed to occur when the cab was in the vicinity of an area of the city bounded by Townsend Lane, Utting Avenue and Priory Road. This obviously didn't make any sense but Alan's mate Eric, who was always reading books about UFOs, reckoned that there was a sort of mini-Bermuda Triangle around Anfield which affected the mechanical workings of the cab.

Alan told him that was ridiculous but, a month later, Alan picked up two young women outside the Grafton nightclub and dropped them off at their home in Arkles Lane in Anfield. As he drove away, he glanced in his rear-view mirror and was startled to see a middle aged man with glasses on, sitting in the back of the cab. Alan stopped the cab and reached for a cosh that he carried under his seat for violent troublemakers.

Then something incredible happened. As soon as Alan demanded "Where are you going mate?" the passenger bowed his head as if he was going to fall asleep and faded away into thousands of little flickering spots. Alan was more stunned than scared. He went into the back of his vehicle to inspect the space where he had just evidently seen a ghost, shook his head and looked around the seats in confusion. A police patrol car turned up and one of the officers asked him what was wrong. Alan said he had just seen a ghost but the policeman just said, "Oh," smirked at his colleague and drove on.

A friend of Brian later told Alan that a passenger had suffered a heart attack in the troublesome cab while the vehicle was travelling up Priory Road. Brian saw the man slump forward and bow his head as he had the attack and he went to help him. Brian realised that the man looked very ill and called out, "Hang on mate, I'll take you to Walton Hospital", but the man had replied, "No, take me home; I'd rather die there. Take me home." The passenger then clutched his chest and died.

Alan asked where the passenger's home had been. "I think it was either Pinehurst Road or Pinehurst Avenue," answered Brian's mate. He knew that it had been Pinehurst something or other. Alan remembered that the cab's steering wheel had turned by itself to go into Pinehurst Road. It seemed as if the ghost had been trying to get the cab to drop its spirit off at home. He told Brian's mate about the incident. "I believe you," said Brian's friend, "that's why Brian sold the cab. It's haunted, but don't say I told you."

Alan later sold that cab to another unsuspecting taxi driver, so that same haunted cab is still on the roads of Liverpool and, if recent accounts are to be believed, the vehicle is still carrying its ghostly home-sick passenger.

Over the Wall

In the 1970s at a house off Liverpool's Myrtle Street, lived Sylvia, a woman of around fifty years of age. She was very nosey, always leaning over the garden wall watching the comings and goings of her neighbours. Sylvia seemed to spend all of her time with her arms folded, resting on the wall and she knew everyone's business. She had few friends but there was one woman called Peggy, who lived in a nearby block of flats called Myrtle Gardens, who often stopped to chat to her.

In 1980, Peggy moved to the Garston area of the city and lost touch with Sylvia. One hot June evening in 1990, Peggy and her husband were driving to a friend's house near the Bluecoat School in the Wavertree area, when Peggy saw Sylvia leaning over a low stone wall, near to a few bushes. Peggy said to her husband, "I don't believe it. It's Sylvia; stop the car."

Peggy's husband stopped and reversed the Volvo estate until he saw Sylvia leaning over the wall in his wing mirror. Peggy got out to talk to her old friend but Peggy's husband had never liked Sylvia and stayed in the car.

"How are you Sylvia?" Peggy asked, looking up at her old friend. The old woman looked as if she had hardly changed.

"Alright. I came here in 1985. Don't like it up here though. It's very secluded," Sylvia replied, with a morose look.

Peggy noticed that her old friend's lips seemed discoloured with a pale blue tinge and she asked her why.

"It's that gas fire. The carbon monoxide affects it. Its probably bad circulation," she replied, sounding very tired. It seemed like an effort just for her to speak.

Peggy felt as if there was a barrier between them because they had not been in touch for so long. Peggy asked her where she lived and Sylvia just nodded to a place on her side of the wall and said, "Over there".

"Church Road? What number? I'll call in sometime," said Peggy and she opened her handbag to find a scrap of paper to write her old friend's address down. Sylvia just shook her head and said, "No it's okay; I don't want any visitors."

Peggy felt ignored and embarrassed. She wrote her phone number down and handed it to Sylvia, saying, "Here's my number; you can give me a call sometime if you want."

Sylvia didn't even take the piece of paper that Peggy offered her, so Peggy placed the bit of paper on the wall. Sylvia just said, "I won't be calling you," and grinned.

Peggy started thinking of an excuse to get back to the car, away from her ignorant friend but Sylvia walked away first without even saying goodbye.

When Peggy got back to the car she told her husband about her old friend's drastic change of personality and he just said he had never liked the woman. Upon turning right at the top of the lane, Peggy and her husband suddenly noticed that there was a church on the corner and next to this church was a graveyard. Sylvia had been leaning over the wall of this graveyard when she had talked to Peggy and this obviously made the couple shiver. Sometime later, they met the vicar of the church and learned that in 1985, Sylvia had been buried near the wall at the spot where Peggy had chatted to her. Peggy nearly fainted when she realised she had been talking to a ghost. Sylvia had died from carbon monoxide poisoning from a faulty gas fire. That explained why she had blue lips.

Married in Haste

This story is one of the strangest ghost stories on record. The following incident has been investigated by writers and researches for over sixty years but no one has ever been able to explain it.

In 1930, a 25-year-old Cheshire woman named Eleanor May was staying with her sister's family in Warwickshire in a little house situated on the periphery of Stratford-upon-Avon. One evening, Eleanor accompanied her sister Emily to a dance that was held in the hall of a local church. The two sisters danced all night and, by midnight, Emily had gone home to her husband, leaving her sister in the arms of a man who said his name was Freddie Barclay. Freddie had receding blond hair, a distinguished aquiline nose, and was quite tall and handsome but he said very little, and seemed a bit shy. He said he was forty and that he worked for a local printer.

Eleanor found herself deeply attracted to Freddie and arranged to meet him at an old country pub called the Magpie and Crown at eight the following Thursday. Freddie walked her home and promised he would be at the pub next week. He kissed her gently and walked away.

The Magpie and Crown was a cosy pub with a thatched roof and a large blazing fire. There are rumours that Shakespeare himself once drank at an old tavern that stood on the same site as the pub in the sixteenth century. At eight o'clock the following Thursday night, Freddie arrived and soon afterwards Eleanor walked in. The couple were soon sitting in the corner, gazing at each other and holding hands.

Freddie and Eleanor met regularly at this pub for about a month until, one evening, Freddie shocked Eleanor and all the drinkers in the pub, by going down on one knee and proposing marriage. Eleanor was surprised but said she would marry him. Although the couple did not have much money, they arranged to marry at the local Church of the Holy Trinity.

Emily was very suspicious about her sister's future husband. He never talked about his home life and just said that he lived with his domineering, old-fashioned mother. He only ever mentioned the area where he lived without actually specifying what his address was. She warned Eleanor to be wary of the printer but Eleanor seemed blinded by her affection for Freddie and said she trusted him.

"For all you know, he could have a wife and children. Bigamy is a serious crime," said Emily.

Eleanor told her sister that she was just jealous, because her own marriage was not succeeding. The outraged Emily told her sister she would certainly not be going to the wedding.

The wedding took place a month later and it was a very simple affair indeed. Only Freddie, Eleanor, the barman from the Magpie and Crown and a few of the other drinkers from the pub were present. Freddie said his mother had been too ill to attend.

After the marriage ceremony, the barman and the drinkers showered the newly-weds with rice and confetti. There was a party back at the Magpie and Crown and this is where events took a sinister turn. During the merrymaking and singing, Eleanor noticed that

Freddie was absent. She asked the barman where he was and he said he had probably gone to the toilet, but Freddie was not in the toilet. In fact, Freddie was nowhere to be seen.

Days went by yet Eleanor refused to take off her wedding dress. She went to her sister and told her what had happened and Emily said, "I told you there was something fishy about him and you attacked me. I've seen all these whirlwind romances before."

Eleanor went to the village police station and told them what had happened. The old sergeant who listened seemed intrigued by Eleanor's account. "You'd better come through," he said, and escorted the young lady into his office, where he sat her down and offered her a drink.

The sergeant told her, "Look Miss. We've heard of this Freddie Barclay before. About ten years back. He did the same thing then. Promised a young lady like yourself that he'd marry her, then vanished."

"I don't understand," said Eleanor.

"Call me superstitious and let it go no further than these four walls, but I reckon this Mr Barclay is a ghost," said the sergeant, solemnly.

"A ghost?" Eleanor recoiled and laughed disbelievingly.

The sergeant remained sombre-faced and said: "I took the liberty on the last occasion of checking up on Freddie Barclay. I discovered that a man of that name and of the same description once worked at a printer's works called Maggs Brothers about a mile away. He was about to marry a girl in the village who, by all accounts, looked like you but she left him at the altar. Unfortunately, Freddie took arsenic and died. His old widowed mother was devastated and she passed away herself soon afterwards from pneumonia brought on by the shock."

"But he was no ghost. He was real. I kissed him," Eleanor told the old policeman.

The sergeant sighed, "That's what the last girl told me. I can't say for certain that he was a ghost. But the last girl who was deserted by Freddie Barclay never saw him again. I showed her his grave in the cemetery outside of the Holy Trinity Church, where you were married."

Eleanor never could accept what the sergeant told her. She never married again and she never heard from the sinister Freddie Barclay.

Weeks after her husband's mysterious disappearance, Eleanor awoke to find her wedding ring was also missing. It was never seen again either.

Eaten Alive

The following grisly account is mentioned in some detail in a fascinating old book called *Days Gone By* by the Victorian folklorist GP Lucas.

In the centre of Liverpool in the late eighteenth century, there stood a bakehouse in a narrow crowded street called Tempest Hey. The proprietor of this bakehouse was an obese man named Andrew Pudsey who took great delight in torturing the many rats and mice that he caught in the cellars of the bakehouse. Pudsey would sometimes take a large carving knife and slice the head off any unfortunate rodent he caught. Often the rat's headless body would run around on the floor for an hour or more. On other occasions, the sadistic baker would get a large skewer and impale a rat or mouse before barbecuing it slowly over an open fire.

On one occasion, he caught a poor skinny-looking mouse and ran a skewer through the little animal's hind-quarters. He then put it high over the flames of the blazing fire and said to a young apprentice named Raymond Smithy, "Listen lad. Listen to its eyes popping." Raymond told fat Pudsey to stop but the cruel baker just grinned and listened with a look of delight as the poor animal squealed in agony.

One sultry evening in August 1792, the Tempest Hey bakehouse was busier than usual because of an order for 800 loaves for the Lord Mayor's banquet. Pudsey and young Raymond worked into the wee small hours to turn out all the bread but the bakers became fatigued by the effort and the unbearable heat so Pudsey decided to have a catnap in the cool cellar. He told Raymond to wake him in an hour's time. Mr Pudsey drank a flagon of cold water, then took his lantern down into the cellar and lay on a pile of sacks that contained flour. He stretched out and yawned and was soon asleep.

Some time later, Pudsey felt something heavy on his chest pressing down. The baker assumed it was Raymond waking him and said, "Alright lad," but when the baker opened his eyes he saw a terrifying sight. An enormous grey rat was on his chest, looking right into his eyes. Pudsey was so terrified, he just closed his eyes and prayed for the enormous rodent to get off him. A few seconds later, the rat hopped off the petrified baker and ran over to a dark corner of the cellar, where there was a huge hole in the wall. This hole had been caused by subsidence and many of the bricks had crumbled away to leave a gaping opening about three feet in diameter. Pudsey had been meaning to brick the hole up but had not got round to it.

The baker took his lantern and went up the stairs and was horrified to see smoke coming from under the trapdoor that led up to the bakehouse. Pudsey could hear the flames crackling and he knew that he could not risk opening the door otherwise the flames would burst through. He panicked and decided that the only way out was through the hole in the cellar. He was obviously scared of meeting the enormous red-eyed rat again, so he peeked into the hole and held the lantern out into the darkness. Several rats in the tunnel ran off in fright and Mr Pudsey started to inch his way through the opening but, because he was so fat, he became stuck. He was jammed tight in the tunnel and started to swear.

Up in the bakehouse, Raymond was lying on the floor, overcome with smoke from the blaze, which had been caused by the overheated oven. A nightwatchman from the building next door broke into the bakehouse and rescued the apprentice but Pudsey was not so lucky. The roof of the cellar started to cave in and fiery chunks of wood and mortar showered the sacks of wheat. Several of the rats hiding in the holes in the cellar panicked and fled towards the large hole which they used as an exit and entrance but Pudsey's fat body was blocking the way. The rats started to nibble and gnaw frantically at the baker's obese body in a desperate effort to escape the flames. The baker's screams were bloodcurdling. One large rat bit and scraped into the baker's buttocks and actually burrowed into the lower intestines of his body. The baker must have suffered an unimaginably agonising death.

The fire was put out an hour later and the body of Andrew Pudsey was recovered. The dead man's face was contorted and twisted in agony and Raymond the apprentice started to cry. The old nightwatchman then pointed to a gaping hole in the corpse's backside where blood was still dripping out. The tip of a rat's tail was visibly dangling out of the hole. Everyone shuddered when a bloodsoaked half-dead rat fall out of the deep gaping wound.

The gruesome tale of the baker who loved to torture rodents does not end there. In 1801, grave diggers in Mulberry Street cemetery had to run for their lives one morning when they unearthed a nest of rats while digging a grave. The rats had been feeding on the corpses in the graveyard and had burrowed a labyrinth of tunnels under the ground. When a ratcatcher smoked out the legion of rodents, the full extent of the damage inflicted by the hungry underground desecrators was seen in its full horror. The contents of one particular coffin had been raided. This was the coffin of Andrew George Pudsey. Even in death he was still fodder for the rats he had once delighted in torturing.

A Haunting Melody

One summer evening in the 1950s, four students from Liverpool went out in a rowing boat off the coast of Llandudno after having a drink. They rowed out to sea for about a quarter of a mile, watching the sun set as they sang a song *Smoke Gets in Your Eyes*, which was in the charts at the time. Another couple who were rowing for the shore in another boat heard the students singing and guessed that they had been drinking. The couple warned them that a storm was on the horizon and looked as if it was coming towards Llandudno. The advice fell on deaf ears and the students just kept singing as they rowed further out to sea.

By nightfall, there was no sign of the students and, suddenly, the storm rolled into Llandudno. Enormous waves broke over the pier and lightning streaked across the skies.

The storm subsided a few hours later and at first light the following morning, an upturned rowing boat was washed up on the beach, along with the body of a young woman. She was one of the students. The other bodies were never found.

About a fortnight later, the couple who had warned the students about the storm, got in a rowing boat and rowed just five hundred yards out into the waters, then opened a small basket containing sandwiches and a bottle of wine. As twilight started to fall, the couple decided to row back to the shore, when they heard something that sent shivers down their spines. They heard the faint strains of the song 'Smoke Gets in Your Eyes', coming from the direction of the sea. As the man started rowing the boat back to the shore, the girl let out a scream and pointed behind him. When the man glanced over his shoulder, he saw the faint silhouette of four people in a rowing boat. As he and his girlfriend looked on, the boat in the distance capsized and screams were heard, followed by a horrible silence as the boat and the figures vanished from sight. The man rowed furiously back to the shore.

A week later, the song was heard again in the lodging house where the students had been staying. The landlady heard the sounds of people coming down her stairs and going out of the front door. However, there were no lodgers occupying her home at this time, so she rushed to the window, and saw the shadows of four people walking by. It is said that the haunting song is still occasionally heard around the month of May off the coast of Llandudno when the wind drops and the sea is calm.

The Mersey Monster

The following story could be compared to a B-movie science fiction film. The sources of this story have been checked and seem genuine but, as ever, it is up to you to draw your own conclusions.

In 1981, a trawler named *Celerity* vanished without a trace in the Irish Sea. It disappeared in broad daylight and no wreckage was ever found. In April the following year, an Irish merchant vessel *Sheralga* was also sunk in the same area of the Irish Sea. The official explanation was that the ship had accidentally snagged her nets on the nuclear sub *HMS Porpoise*.

Witnesses said this did not seem to be the case at all and several horrified fishermen watched the doomed ship being pulled backwards by something in the water for an incredible distance of ten nautical miles. *Sheralga* then capsized but the crew were incredibly lucky. They jumped overboard and were rescued by passing trawlers.

On the same day in the same area, another fishing vessel *Crimson Dawn* was spreading its nets when some massive object the size of a whale became entangled in the nets. *Crimson Dawn* was dragged along like a toy boat by the unidentified thing and only escaped being dragged beneath the waves when the nets snapped. Months later, in the same area, another fishing vessel named *Galvanor* mysteriously disappeared beneath the waves, along with its crew of eight.

A year afterwards, another ship *Cite D'Aleth* literally sank in seconds off the Irish coast of Wexford, taking ten men with her and months after that unexplained tragedy, two British trawlers, *Zanto* and *Exuberant* shared the same mysterious fate. Many more fishing vessels have been dragged under the waves of the Irish sea since the 1980s, but is there a common cause behind the plethora of sinister maritime tragedies?

A concerned pressure group called the Celtic League has compiled a dossier containing a long catalogue of bizarre incidents that have occurred in a small area of the Irish Sea and presented it to the Government. Nuclear sub activity is often blamed and may well be the explanation but there have been rumours and whispers that something much more unusual is behind all the sinkings of the trawlers in the area.

Several radio hams who regularly eavesdrop on military wavebands claim that there is a large sea creature prowling in the Irish Sea. This outlandish claim has strangely been backed up by leaks from people who worked in the Faslane nuclear submarine base in Scotland. Staff at the base have claimed that the navy sent three Polaris subs to specific areas of the Irish sea and even to Liverpool Bay to search for the enormous sea monster, fitting the classic description of the fabled Loch Ness monster.

In 1989, one radio ham claimed that he heard a chilling conversation between the crews of two nuclear subs on the very-low frequency band. The captain of one of the subs said, "The thing is now moving south west towards Liverpool Bay. Can you see it yet?"

A dramatic reply came back from a communications officer on the other sub. He said, "Ten-sixty-nine. We have collided with it. That thing is longer than us and is heading to the [Mersey] estuary near the north-east of the [Wirral] peninsula." The sub radio operator then said that the submarine ran a risk of grounding in shallow waters and was therefore returning to a pre-planned rendezvous point.

There have been sightings of a huge long-necked creature in the waters of the Irish sea that date back to the early 1900s. The last recent sightings were in the mid-1960s, when two men on board the Liverpool to Dublin ferry spotted the creature moving at 30 knots through the waters of Liverpool Bay, about ten miles north of Prestatyn. Although both men were seasoned mariners, their reports were not taken seriously.

For over two centuries, the Welsh fishermen of Cardigan Bay have claimed that a sea serpent patrols the Irish Sea and the Cornish fishermen also claim that a sea monster they call 'Morgwar' also roams the same waters. Some think that the Welsh and Cornish sea monster are one and the same, because their descriptions are identical. Both are said to have a long neck with a greyish green body. Such a creature was allegedly seen chasing a baby whale near Hilbre Island off the coast of Hoylake in 1901.

Some think that when the Mersey becomes cleaner, the sea creature may even swim up the river and ground itself on the banks just like whales once did.

Lightning Persecution

There is an old but incorrect saying that 'Lightning never strikes in the same place twice'. In fact, there are many park rangers in America's Yellowstone Park who have been struck more than three times by lightning while patrolling the wide open parkland and some have been killed by the searing bolts of electricity. Nearer to us, in North Wales, there was one unfortunate man who was literally victimised by lightning in the middle of the last century.

In 1857, Horace Pym, the twenty year-old son of Sir Walter Pym, a wealthy landowner and ruthless businessman, left his family's sprawling mansion on the outskirts of St Asaph. He rode on horseback around the Welsh countryside, until he spotted a beautiful Welsh girl named Megan, who was standing on a hill, throwing corn to the birds. Horace Pym rode up to Meg and dismounted. He told the girl he was the son of Sir Walter but the girl could hardly understand English. Horace thought she was ignoring him, and raised his hand to the girl. Megan flinched but Horace did not hit her. He enjoyed the way the girl looked so afraid of him and relished the moment. The girl cried out something in Welsh and a bird of prey that resembled a falcon swooped down and attacked the young man. Horace fell to the ground and rolled down the hill. The girl shouted out some more words in her native tongue and Pym's horse bolted out of the area. Pym then assaulted the girl. Some accounts say that he also raped her.

As Pym turned away, Meg started crying and pointed to the skies and started shouting something Pym could not understand. As he ran off, the clouds overhead darkened and soon it was raining heavily. Thunder rumbled through the hills and, suddenly, a bolt of forked lightning struck him. The bolt pierced his scalp and burnt holes in his feet. Pym fell to the ground, unconscious. When he awoke it was night and he felt seriously ill.

When he reached home, he told his father he had been attacked by Welsh peasants who had tried to rob him. Pym's father was furious and sent a group of men armed with shotguns to the area but all they found was young Megan and her mother, who lived in a run-down cottage. One of Pym's men knew that Megan and her mother were regarded as witches and left them well alone. Megan's mother Sian, was known throughout the valleys as a horse-whisperer; someone who could communicate with the animals and beasts of burden. She had evidently taught her magical gift to her daughter, who had been seen talking to foxes and birds.

The men returned to their master's estate and told Sir Walter there were no peasants in the area where young Horace said he had been attacked. Sir Walter hit his son with a riding whip and ordered him to stay in his quarters in the mansion for a week.

A few days later, a terrible thunderstorm descended on St Asaph and ravaged Sir Walter's estate. Several of his men were killed by the lightning and during the fearful storm, young Horace hid under his bed, terrified of being struck by lightning again. When the storm calmed, Horace went to the window and peeped out at the clouds. A powerful flash of sheet lightning zapped his face, temporarily blinding him. The surge of electrical energy was of such ferocity, it actually scorched an image of Horace's face on the window pane. This 'lightning picture' as it became known, remained etched on the window until the mansion was demolished in 1900.

Horace was later sent to Preston to supervise his father's printing business and died a year later after falling from his horse in 1860. A week after his burial, a thunderstorm raged over Preston and a bolt of lightning shattered Horace Pym's gravestone. Even in death, he was still victimised by the vengeful forks of electricity.

The Finger of Suspicion

In 1812, Duncan McPhail, a poor baker in the Everton district of Liverpool, was struggling financially. A rival baker in the same district was selling his bread at a cheaper price and had a team of hard-working delivery boys. The rival baker was rapidly driving McPhail out of business, so the latter decided to resort to a life of crime.

He visited a graveyard in Mulberry Street, Edge Hill, in the dead of night, equipped with a spade and a lantern and dug into the grave of a local doctor who was rumoured to have been buried with his jewellery. McPhail took an hour to smash through the coffin lid but saw to his delight that the doctor's hands had gold rings on almost every finger and in the silk-lined coffin there was a silver snuff box, a solid gold pendant and a gold watch and chain. McPhail prised each of the stiff fingers of the corpse open, slipped off the rings, then snatched all the doctor's personal treasures.

The first rays of the sun were appearing on the eastern horizon, so McPhail clambered out of the hole without even bothering to cover it up.

A week later, McPhail returned to the graveyard but was almost caught by a nightwatchman who saw his lantern among the gravestones. McPhail decided that grave-robbery was dangerous and too physically demanding, so he resorted to robbery with violence. Dressed in black, with a black silk scarf covering the lower half of his face, McPhail waited in dark alleyways in the town after midnight, hoping to pounce on any vulnerable drunk who looked affluent enough to be worth coshing.

He found such a victim when Samuel Jones, a cotton merchant, came staggering from a tavern which stood in a street that is now Pembroke Place. McPhail crept up behind the drunken merchant and delivered a succession of heavy blows with a weighted stick to the back of the man's head. Blood showered the robber during the attack and his scarf fell off. After dragging Jones into the alleyway, McPhail emptied the victim's pockets of money and ripped off his watch and chain. McPhail then saw that Jones's eyes were wide open and lifeless. He was now a murderer. Suddenly, the voice of an old woman cried out in the darkness, "You've killed him!"

McPhail panicked and searched the alleyway, determined to silence his only witness, but when he failed to find her, he ran off into the night.

The following morning, two detectives and a soldier arrested McPhail on a charge of murdering Samuel Jones and they presented their witness: the old woman in the alleyway who had seen the brutal killing. The old sinister-looking woman, who was dressed in a black funeral shawl, said, "His shoes and arms were covered in blood."

McPhail laughed and pointed to his shoes and arms. He had cleaned the blood away. He had also hid the money he had taken from Jones. The detectives were about to admit defeat, when the old woman said she was a gypsy and knew how to identify a murderer. She said that if she uttered an old spell, the corpse would point to the person who had taken its life. The detectives agreed to the woman's idea and ordered McPhail to the mortuary where the covered body of Samuel Jones was lying on a slab. Already, McPhail was twitching with nerves as he kept protesting his innocence.

Suddenly, the woman recited three phrases in an unknown language, then in a loud voice said, "Samuel Jones, here you lie, point to the one who caused you to die."

After about five seconds, the corpse's arm twitched and slowly rose from under the sheet covering it and its pale index finger pointed at McPhail. The murderer moved about nervously and the finger moved around too, pointing at him.

The detectives wore expressions of terror and disbelief. McPhail gave a little feigned laugh and said "I know how it's done. Someone's under the sheet playing on my wits." McPhail grabbed the sheet, thinking the detectives and the fake gypsy were idiots for trying to stage such a charade. He pulled the sheet away and there was the lifeless body of Samuel Jones. His hair was crimson with dried blood; his face was bruised black, blue and yellow and his eyes were still open but the eyeballs were white.

As McPhail screamed out, the arm dropped. The baker tried to run out of the room but was apprehended by the detectives and made to dictate all the deplorable events he had committed, including the murder of Samuel Jones. McPhail then signed his statement and, a month later, he was hanged on the gallows at Kirkdale. The old gypsy woman mysteriously disappeared after the execution and was never seen again.

Phantoms of the Sky

The skies over the north-west have been the backdrop to many strange incidents over the years. Since the 1950s, a phantom plane has been heard droning over the Speke area. It is usually heard in the evenings when there is low cloud and many believe the ghostly aircraft is a German World War Two bomber that crashed into the Mersey after being shot down in the early 1940s.

Another spectral plane is seen regularly buzzing the skies of Southport during twilight hours. The plane is a Cessna light-aircraft and has been seen by scores of people, including policemen, since May 1989. One night, the ghostly pilot nose-dived his aircraft into a marsh near Crossens in Southport and residents in the area jammed the switchboards of the local police station and Speke Airport. The police closed the Southport coastal road and the emergency services rushed to the site of the crash but there was no trace of any wreckage. Stranger still, the same eerie white plane was seen performing the very same nose-dive into the marsh on the following night; only then did the local residents realise that they were witnessing a ghostly plane crash.

About a year before, an identical Cessna light-aircraft smashed onto the beach in Southport. The pilot, who had just been jilted by his girlfriend, committed suicide by performing a nose-dive manoeuvre into the sands. Some think that this explains the ghost-plane's suicidal dive into the marsh.

In May 1996, a stranger incident was experienced in broad daylight by three pilots as they flew through the skies over Speke airport.

A pilot named Dave was circling the area near Speke Airport at around seven thousand feet in a light-aircraft when, out of the corner of his eye, he saw something fall from the clear blue sky. When Dave turned his head to see what it was, he was astonished to see that it was a human figure plummeting to earth. What was even stranger was the fact that the sky-diver wore a pair of orange wings. Behind the bizarre-looking winged figure, Dave could see a parachute trailing. The chute had not opened fully, and just flapped about as the stranger fell faster and faster to the airfield thousands of feet below.

Dave strained to look out the side window of his aircraft and saw the terrible impact. With a mounting sense of horror at being the witness to a fatal parachute jump, Dave radioed the emergency services and gave them the location where the winged man had smashed into the ground.

When the emergency services arrived at the airfield, they could not find any dead parachutist. There was nothing there at all. Dave was interviewed at length by the police and they told him that another pilot who had flown in from Cheshire on the day before had also reported seeing a man fall from the sky but, again, no one could find his body.

A helicopter pilot saw the same ghostly figure falling from a clear blue sky a week later. The figure wore a pair of wings and landed in the same airfield. On this occasion, a friend of the chopper pilot looked at the figure on the ground below with binoculars and could clearly see a man lying spread-eagled in the field with long streaks of blood flowing from him. Next to the body was a fluttering parachute that had only partially opened. Close to the corpse were the splintered remains of what seemed to be yellowish-orange wooden wings. The helicopter dived down so the pilot and his mate could take a closer look at the parachutist but he was no longer there.

No one wanted to enquire into the incident any further and the pilots who witnessed the falling man decided not to make an official statement for understandable reasons.

So who was the winged sky-diver? Research has established that exactly forty years before, on 21 May, 1956, a thirty-seven year-old Frenchman named Leo Valentin leaped from a small plane over Speke Airport. He wore two parachutes and a pair of wooden wings and intended to glide through the skies over south Liverpool. Because it was Whit Monday, thousands of people turned out to witness the spectacular stunt but instead, the crowds screamed in horror when the Frenchman fell to his death.

Leo Valentin jumped out of the plane and accidentally clipped one of his wings on the hatchway. He then hit the tail of the plane and the wing splintered. The French Birdman then went into a dramatic spin and lost control. After falling one thousand feet, he pulled the ripcord but his chute did not open properly. He pulled the cord of the emergency chute but that did not work either and the skydiver fell to his death from a height of eight thousand feet. He hit the ground with a loud thud and hundreds of children and women screamed and started to cry as the Frenchman's blood sprayed everywhere. The spread-eagled corpse lay there with its broken wings nearby and the partly opened parachute fluttered about in the breeze like a shroud. The airfield is the very same one where Dave and the other two pilots saw the falling man hit the ground.

According to rumours, the spectre of Leo Valentin is supposedly still seen falling from the sky over Speke Airport.

The Real Jekyll and Hyde

Most people have heard or read of Robert Louis Stevenson's disturbing tale of dual personality, *The Strange Case of Dr Jekyll and Mr Hyde*, which was first published in 1886. Some think that Stevenson based his story on the double life of Edinburgh's Deacon Brodie, who was a respectable businessman by day and a vicious thief by night. But there was also a real-life Jekyll and Hyde character at large in Liverpool in the mid-nineteenth century.

Richard Rawlins was a fairly wealthy engineer who had shares in several Cornish tin mines and the Liverpool to Manchester Railway. He was said to be a tall, dark, handsome man with a fine voice and a rather shrewd nature. He had married three times, each marriage ending after a year because of Rawlins' dramatic mood swings and strange dual personality.

From his childhood, Richard Rawlins claimed he had a naughty 'twin' inside him named Ralph. The young child even changed hands to write and draw when he became Ralph. Ralph was a nasty, mischievous personality who delighted in pulling the legs off spiders and Richard was a nice boy who picked flowers for his mother. It was Richard's mother who had unwittingly christened Richard's 'twin', after her son had told her about the imaginary double who lived inside him. Richard called his alter ego 'the other fellow', but Mrs Rawlins suggested the name Ralph, which had been her grandfather's name.

A children's doctor was baffled at the child's split personality disorder and surmised it was just young Richard's way of getting attention. However, in adolescence, Richard became Ralph more often, usually when he had undergone an emotional time or had been involved in an accident.

When sixteen year-old Richard broke up with his girlfriend Lottie, he broke down in tears in Toxteth Park. A policeman approached the distressed young man and asked him what was the matter. The rejected Romeo's angelic face became twisted and his eyes squinted at the police officer. Richard had become Ralph and he spat in the policeman's face and ran out of the park shouting abuse at passers-by. Upon reaching his home in Duke Street, the mentally unstable teenager was attacked by his dog Samson, a huge black Labrador. The dog loved Richard but growled and ran from the boy when he 'became' Ralph.

The teenager ran into the front parlour and suffered a fit. He was found by the maid, biting into the hearth rug and foaming at the mouth. As the maid called for Richard's father, the boy passed out. When he was revived with smelling salts, he told his parents that Ralph had spat at a policeman and had screamed abuse at people in the street on his way home. The weeks went by without Ralph appearing and the boy seemed normal enough. Only occasionally did he swap his pen to his left hand when he wrote and even then there were only minor variations in the teenager's handwriting style. As the years passed, it looked as if the rebellious Ralph had disappeared forever into the depths of Richard Rawlins' subconscious. But in 1845, a dramatic accident brought Ralph back into Richard's life with a vengeance.

Richard Rawlins was now a twenty-five-year-old mining engineer who patented several explosive devices for blasting quarries and mines. On 1 November 1845, Rawlins entered the Dale Street premises of Rodney Hart, a gunsmith and gunpowder supplier. Rawlins intended to purchase five pounds of gunpowder to test out a detonation device he was working on for the mines. Whilst he was there, a young apprentice in the cellar of the shop dropped a flintlock he had just loaded and the gun went off, blasting a hole in a barrel of gunpowder. The apprentice was killed instantly and only parts of his body were later found. The shop-owner Rodney Hart was blown through the windows of the premises but survived. Richard Rawlins was blown up onto the first floor of the devastated shop by the tremendous force of the blast. He was found hanging over a beam, barely alive, suffering from concussion.

He was treated at his Duke Street home by several distinguished physicians from a Rodney Street surgery and, for a week, it looked as if the young man would remain in a comatose state. Amazingly, he pulled through or, at least, Ralph pulled through. Richard's personality was evidently destroyed in the shop explosion.

As soon as the young man was able to get out of his bed, he practically raped his maid and then assaulted the cook who was a sixty year-old woman. Ralph stole over one hundred guineas from his father's room and then escaped by climbing dangerously out of a garret window. He ran across the rooftops and went on a crime spree, committing two burglaries in the Islington district, sexually assaulting three young women in Everton and almost battering a pub landlord to death because the ale he served was slightly sour.

Unlike the meek Richard, Ralph had the strength of a savage and seemed to take delight in battling with the police. The wayward Ralph Rawlins was finally cornered in Vauxhall Road a week later by eight policemen armed with batons. The mixed-up young man had just set fire to a soap warehouse and the damage was estimated to be almost one thousand pounds.

Sadly, a blow on the skull from a policeman's riot baton killed Ralph instantly. The man with two personalities suffered a haemorrhage of the brain and died with blood gushing from his nose and ears. Surgeons at the Liverpool Medical Institute in Mount Pleasant were eager to get to the bottom of the dead man's double personality and sought permission to open his skull up. At first Ralph's father refused permission, but later had a change of heart, as he too was curious to learn about his son's illness.

A surgeon sawed open the skull of the young man and was flabbergasted by what he saw: there were two brains tightly pressed together in the skull case, or four hemispherical lobes in all. The surgeon surmised that Richard was meant to have been one half of a twin when he was conceived. The other twin never developed into an embryo but retained its brain, which grew alongside the brain of its twin.

Undoubtedly, one of the brains contained the personality of Richard and the other brain was the spiteful counterpart which asserted itself as Ralph. The Rawlins family naturally did not want society to know of their freakish son, so the findings of the Medical Institute were filed away for posterity.

King of the Dock Road

The following true story must rank as one of the blackest comedies in the history of Liverpool.

In the year 1870, there was an disreputable public house situated on the waterfront near to Mann Island called the Black Horse, where the shady villains of Liverpool's underworld used to congregate. According to legend, the landlord of this squalid watering hole was a direct descendant of Dick Turpin, the famous highwayman. This legend was once thought to be nonsense but it is now known that Turpin actually visited Liverpool with his fellow rogue Tom King in the early 1730s whilst on the run.

The landlord who said he was Turpin's descendant was Joe Tyler and he called himself 'King of the Dock Road'. Any thieves or burglars caught operating on his manor were brought before him and faced two options: either they joined his establishment and gave him half of their loot or they were turned over to the police.

One day, in January 1870, an unfortunate burglar from another area made the mistake of breaking into the Black Horse at four in the morning. Joe Tyler came downstairs after hearing a tinkle of glass breaking and caught the burglar, who was John Peters, aged just thirteen. Peters was halfway through the window when Tyler grabbed hold of him. He called his wife downstairs and held the youth with a revolver to his head. Lizzie Tyler came down in her nightgown and when she saw the young burglar, she told her husband, "Give him a good hiding then let him go home with a sore backside. Here, I'll give the cheeky beggar a good spanking myself!"

"Get away woman!" Joe said, and pulled the boy by his hair to the cellar. Joe told his wife to get some rope and something to gag the boy with.

The boy was held at gunpoint in the cellar among the barrels of beer while Lizzie bound him up with rope.

"Tie him up tighter than that! Don't mollycoddle him!" Joe told his wife.

"Ah, but he's just a child and a nice looking one at that," said Lizzie sympathetically.

"Never pity a thief, Lizzie. They'll rob your eyes and spit in the sockets if you feel sorry for them. He was trying to rob the place remember," said Joe.

Lizzie thought about her husband's words then tightened the rope, saying, "Little blighter!"

"What's your name?" Joe asked the little criminal.

"John Smith," replied the kid, nervously.

Joe Tyler ran over to him and pointed the revolver between his eyes, "Don't lie to Joe Tyler! I'm the King of the Dock Road, and no one lies to me."

"Yeah, no one lies to Joe, not even me," said Lizzie, adding, "His great grandfather was Dick Turpin, y'know."

"So tell me who you are or I'll shoot you and they'll be finding your bones in this cellar in a hundred years," Joe demanded.

"My name's John Peters," whimpered the little burglar, ready to cry.

"Good," said Joe, smiling. "Now, lad why did you try to break into my place?"

The boy shrugged.

"Don't shrug at me or I'll break your collar bone," Joe warned him pointing his gun at the boy. "Someone put you up to it didn't they?"

"No sir," sobbed the boy.

Joe Tyler was paranoid and thought that crooks from other areas of the city were trying to move onto his patch. He was convinced that the boy had been sent to break into the pub to make him look like an incompetent fool, so Joe slapped the boy's face and growled, "Who sent you?"

The boy blurted out, "I don't know his name but he had a beard and moustache and a mole on his face."

"That's more like it boy!" said Joe, strutting up and down the cellar, wondering who the bearded man was. Suddenly, there was a heavy knocking at the door of the pub and a voice shouted, "Police! Open up!"

Joe Tyler's legs turned to jelly. He had stolen property stacked in the upstairs rooms of the pub so he hid the revolver and told his wife to gag the child while he went up to answer the door.

When he opened the door, he found two tall policemen peering in through the broken window. "Hello constables," said Joe innocently. As they asked him if everything was alright, Lizzie let out a loud scream in the cellar. The little burglar had deliberately brought his bound feet down heavily on her foot. The policemen ordered Tyler to open the door and when they went downstairs, they saw the boy tied up. Tyler explained what had happened and the police took the boy away, warning Tyler not to take the law into his own hands next time.

The following night, Joe Tyler and his mob waited until an old caretaker named Bob Woods came into the pub. He had a beard and moustache and a mole on his face, so they reckoned that he had to be the instigator who had sent John Peters to break into the pub. When Woods walked in and asked for a beer, Joe Tyler gave the nod and two of his men threw a sack over Woods' head and took him down to the cellar. Most of the drinkers were criminals and they all went to the cellar, excitedly waiting for the kangaroo court to begin.

Joe Tyler sat on his specially made, high-backed chair and presided over the makeshift court as Woods had his hands tied behind his back and was cross-questioned about his attempts to make Tyler and his men a laughing stock. Woods ended up crying and saying that he wanted to go home but Tyler decided to play his old trick of ordering the accused to be executed by a tall muscular man who wore a black hood with two eye-holes. Woods was blindfolded and made to bend over with his head on a chopping block.

The executioner lifted a mop with a wet head over Woods and Joe said solemnly, "Bob Woods, you have been found guilty of trying to undermine the prestige of Joe Tyler and his associates and of instigating burglary so, as you refuse to admit your guilt, I hereby sentence you to have your head chopped off. Go ahead, executioner!"

The crowd of crooks looking on pretended to cry out in horror and watched poor Bob Woods shaking. The executioner grinned and handed the mop to Joe Tyler. Tyler brought down the mop; its wet head slapped hard against the nape of Woods' neck and everyone laughed but Bob lay there motionless. He had a weak heart and had died from shock.

The criminals soon deserted Tyler and two of them who secretly hated him informed the police. Meanwhile, John Peters said he had made his story about a bearded man up because he thought Tyler was going to kill him if he stayed silent and said nothing.

Tyler went on the run for two days while police searched the area. He hid in a dock warehouse, then boarded a ship City of Boston at Liverpool Docks under an assumed name. The ship sailed for New York where the self-styled 'King of the Dock Road' probably dreamt of setting himself up in business and crime. But, alas, history records that the ship Tyler boarded was lost at sea.

Night Terror

This is a bizarre story to keep you awake at nights and it took place at Moreton in July 1863. Stewart Parker, a retired hangman, was sitting in bed next to his wife reading a book, when he fell asleep. The time was just after one o'clock in the morning.

An hour later, Mrs Parker woke up and turned in the bed to see her husband fighting for his breath. He was drenched in sweat and was making choking noises. She shouted his name repeatedly but he would not wake up. This naturally worried Mrs Parker. Her husband had a weak heart and he seemed so afraid of the nightmare he was having that it looked as if he would die with fear.

The frightened woman slapped her husband across the face but to no avail. As a last resort, she poured a glass of water over his face and shook him violently. His eyes flew open and he seemed to be paralysed for a few moments. Then he grabbed at his throat and in a raspy dry voice said, "Thank God – it was just a dream."

Mrs Parker said she thought he was gone for a moment and asked him what he had been dreaming of. He told her, "I dreamt that a man in a black hood came forward. I asked him who he was and he said Peter Woods."

"Who is he?" asked Mrs Parker.

Her husband looked worried, "An old housebreaker who was hanged for the murder of a widow in Ashton town. After he was hanged, the real murderer was caught and confessed. Peter Woods said he'd return to haunt me, the jury and the judge. He said he had gypsy blood in him."

"Oh, it was just a nightmare," said Mrs Parker and she shook her head when she saw the wet patch she had caused with the glass of water.

"But it was a horrible dream, dear," replied her husband and he told her the rest of the dream. "Woods tied my hands behind me and put a strap round my ankles. He then pushed me so I was standing on the trapdoors of a gallows. Just as he put the noose over my head, you woke me up. I'm not that keen to go back to sleep now."

"Oh don't be so silly. You ate toasted cheese before you went to bed, didn't you?" said Mrs Parker.

"Yes, but I've never had a nightmare so vivid and so real before," replied Mr Parker.

"Cheese does that," said his wife. "It's well known that cheese upsets the brain when you sleep."

Half an hour later, Mr Parker fell asleep and, at around half past three, his wife woke to hear a strange snoring sound. It was her husband having another dream. This time she had to push him out of bed and roll him across the floor to wake him. He got up, gasped for air and threw the window open so he could inhale the fresh air.

"Are you alright? Shall I call a doctor?" asked the concerned Mrs Parker.

"No. It was Woods again," gasped Mr Parker. "He tried to hang me again. This time the trapdoor opened. I fell through the trapdoor and was hanging but you woke me in time. Am I going insane?"

By twenty to five the couple were drowsy and were already laughing at the ordeal and now Mr Parker really did seem ready for a good night's sleep. He kissed his wife, rolled over and went straight to sleep. The next morning at eight o'clock, his wife woke up to find him dead. His face was purple and the veins in his face were sticking out. His eyes were open and seemed to be bulging out of their sockets. Mrs Parker let out a scream and ran to her sister in the next street. Her sister summoned a doctor who, after examining Mr Parker stated that he had died of a heart attack brought on by what is known as 'night terror', a very traumatic nightmare in which the dreamer is unable to wake up. Night terror is rare, but there are around ten cases reported in England each year.

The pathologist who performed the post mortem on the old hangman's body was baffled by a reddish band around Mr Parker's neck. Such a mark was often found on the necks of condemned criminals who had been hanged. It was caused by rope-burn from the noose. The coroner could not explain the mark and surmised it was produced by haemorrhaging of the blood vessels in the neck caused by the coronary, but when Mrs Parker saw the strange mark on her deceased husband's neck, she knew that Peter Woods had somehow exacted his revenge.

Break-in at the Ghost House

The following strange incident was investigated by the old West Lancashire police force, back in the days before the Merseyside force was formed.

It was Autumn, 1966. A dense blanket of thick fog rolled across the north west, causing many fatal car accidents. The fog did not lift for three days and one night during this murky period, two petty burglars named Richard and Carl decided to prowl around Maghull, which lies on the northern outskirts of Liverpool.

The two criminals decided to take advantage of the fog and tiptoed to a cottage near the village of Lunt. However, an Alsatian dog chased the two men after the flu-stricken Richard sneezed, so they decided to scout around in another area. The burglars finally found the type of place they were looking for at half past two in the morning on the outskirts of Ince Blundell. It was a magnificent Elizabethan-style mansion and it stood in the middle of a secluded field near the bottom of a hill.

Richard and Carl sneaked up the path to the huge oak door of the large house and Richard read the plate, which said 'Magpie House' in delicate gold letters. Richard took out a hanky and blew his nose. His flu was getting worse and the cold foggy night was not helping it.

Carl peeped through the windows and said, "Cor, look at the gear in there, Richie. It's like an Aladdin's Cave."

"It's probably alarmed. Be careful," said Richard as he took out a roll of sticky tape and looked about. After tearing six strips of the tape and sticking them across the window, he wrapped a piece of cloth around the crowbar he carried and tapped the window gently until the pane cracked and fragmented. Richard gently peeled away the strips of tape with the pieces of the window that were stuck to it and Carl reached in through the hole in the windowpane and grabbed the handle. He turned it, pulling the window wide open. Both men waited tensely, expecting an alarm to go off but there was just silence.

The burglars climbed into the house and located two silver candlesticks with candles in them on the marble mantelpiece. Richard took out his lighter and lit the candles. Both thieves took one and surveyed what seemed to be the parlour. A huge framed oil painting of a rural country scene in the style of Constable hung over the fireplace but it was too large to carry out of the house. Richard and Carl sneaked into the hall and went upstairs to another room, passing a spooky suit of armour on the stairs. In this room there was a grand piano and several smaller oil paintings. Richard removed the paintings and carried them under his arm while Carl ransacked a cabinet in the corner It contained no money, so the thieves continued on their robbing expedition. In another room, Carl grabbed another pair of solid silver candlesticks and Richard grabbed a small ornamental gold clock.

Suddenly, a strange noise sounded in the house which stopped the thieves in their tracks.

"What was that?" whispered Carl, his eyes darting about anxiously.

"Ssshhh!" Richard listened intensely. "Sounds like someone snoring upstairs. Let's go and have a look."

"No way, let's get out of here. We've got enough," said Carl who was extremely nervous now.

"Pull yourself together," Richard snapped. "Look, the toffs usually have all their valuables and jewellery in their bedrooms. So let's go and have a look. Don't start turning yellow now."

"Come on, Richie, don't be greedy. We've got enough," complained Carl.

But Richard grabbed his friend by the arm and pulled him as he ascended the stairway to the bedrooms.

Richard heard the snoring sound getting louder and he smiled as he slowly turned the handle of the bedroom door. Ever so gently, he pushed the door open and saw an old man lying in bed, snoring in the depths of deep sleep. The man looked very old-fashioned and quaint. He wore a pointed nightcap with a bobbin at the end and had a huge droopy walrus moustache. The bed he slept in was an old four-poster, but what alarmed the burglars was that the old man was sleeping with an old-fashioned blunderbuss gun which had a ridiculous cone shaped barrel. The old man embraced the gun as if he cherished the weapon. Upon seeing the gun, Carl said, "That's it, Richie, I'm quitting here right now, pronto."

"Wait a minute, you coward, look," whispered Richard and he pointed to a rusty metal box under the four-poster bed. "That's got to be his savings or something. We can't quit now. We're so near. That old geezer's probably too deaf to hear Gabriel's Horn." Richard's greed got the better of him. With the clock under his arm he sneaked across the room towards the bed, one agonising step at a time, each step seeming like an eternity. Carl remained rooted to the spot in the doorway, holding the stolen candlesticks and several small paintings.

Richard knelt down near the four poster and carefully dragged the metal box from under the bed. He put the clock down and prised off the lid and there was every burglar's dream: a hoard of gold coins mixed up with a treasure of silver and gold rings. Suddenly, the clock Richard had taken from downstairs started to chime three o'clock. It was a moment of sheer terror. On the first chime, Richard ducked under the bed, and the man mumbled something in his sleep. On the second chime the old man put his finger on the trigger of the blunderbuss and upon the final chime he shouted out, "Damn clock! Be quiet."

He started snoring again, so Richard got up with sweat trickling in his eyes and picked up the metal box with both hands. He stood up, turned around, then looked at Carl, who was also perspiring with nerves. Richard crept across the room and nodded at the treasure in the box he carried. He stopped walking and closed his eyes, then his nose twitched, the burglar opened his mouth; he was about to sneeze.

"No," muttered Carl, anticipating the noise his friend was about to produce.

"Aaaaashhooooo!!!" Richard let out a loud sneeze and the old man shot up in the bed like a jack-in-the-box. He saw the intruders and took aim with his blunderbuss and blasted Richard in the backside. The burglar dropped the metal box and the coins and countless rings scattered everywhere. The burglars ran down the stairs as fast as their legs could carry them and, on the way, Carl dropped the paintings and the silver candlesticks. The two frightened men leaped out the open ground-floor window into the foggy night and ran and ran until they were out of breath.

Richard went to hospital to have the buckshot removed from his behind and a suspicious doctor alerted the police. Detectives turned up at the hospital and questioned Richard. A detective said that Richard would not get the buckshot removed until he told them what he had been involved in. The burglar was in agony, so he confessed to the housebreaking attempt.

The Police were baffled, for when they went to the spot where Magpie House had stood, there was nothing but old ruins. A local farmer told the police that the old ruins were the remains of Magpie House, which had been demolished in 1910. It seemed that the burglars had broken into a ghostly house and understandably, the police discontinued their investigation.

Old Bob

The following incident took place in Liverpool in 1988 and was witnessed by four people, including a policewoman.

In November 1987, Irene, a fifty-two year-old woman, had a minor stroke which left her partially paralysed down her left side, which meant that she had difficulty walking. Her fourteen year-old daughter Carla looked after her mum outside school hours but Irene refused to have a helper in her home. She was too proud and so she hobbled about the house with a walking stick.

In the summer of 1988, Carla had a chance to go on holiday to France with her school, but was worried that her mother would be unable to cope without her help. Irene insisted that her daughter should go on the trip and told her that the effects of the stroke were wearing off and that she was improving each day. That night, Carla burst into tears and hugged her mum saying, "I'll stay with you mum, it wouldn't feel right having a good time in France while you're suffering here."

"Don't be silly, Carla," said Irene hugging her daughter. "You're going to France. You deserve a break after looking after me all the time. Is that a deal?" Carla sniffled and nodded. By the following week she was holidaying in the south of France with her schoolfriends.

Irene felt very uneasy about being in the house on her own without her daughter and looked forward to Carla's phonecall from France to tell her she was well. One morning at three o'clock, Irene awoke hearing a rattling noise coming from downstairs. She initially thought it was Carla returning from holiday but when Irene got out of bed and limped to the window, she froze with fear. Two tall men with black ski hats on were attempting to break in. One was standing at the gate in the front of the house keeping watch, while his colleague was forcing the door open with a small crow bar.

Irene's heart began to pound with terror; she had to phone the police but as she did not have a phone in her bedroom, she would have to get to the phone downstairs in the hall before the thugs broke in. As she opened her bedroom door, she heard a splintering, cracking sound, then heard the front door fly open and a stranger's deep voice saying "Hurry up!"

Irene almost fainted with fear as the burglars came into the house. She shouted out to an imaginary husband, "John! There's someone downstairs!" but the burglars laughed and took no notice. They had been keeping watch on the house and knew Irene was a practically housebound invalid with no husband. The sound of heavy footsteps pounded on the stairs and one of the tall burglars demanded, "You stupid cow! Come here!"

Irene staggered back into her bedroom, closed the door behind her and leaned against it. She whispered, "Please God, don't let him in!" Suddenly, there was a loud growling noise and Irene heard the burglar cry out and fall down the stairs. There were more growling noises and the sound of a dog barking. A blue flash of light lit up the bedroom as a police patrol car and police van arrived at the scene of the burglary. Irene looked out of the window and watched the two burglars run straight into the arms of the policemen outside. Once the men had been apprehended, one of the policemen entered the house to reassure Irene. He said a neighbour had phoned them after seeing the burglars trying to break into her home.

The policeman then said, "I think your dog's done a runner, love." Irene looked puzzled.

"Your dog. There's no sign of it. Don't worry, it'll come back," the policeman continued.

"I haven't got a dog officer," said Irene and she recalled the strange growling noise she had heard when the burglars had entered the house.

"One of the rogues down there has got a big bite on his backside. He said your Alsatian went for him," the policeman explained.

"But I swear, officer, I haven't got a dog," said Irene. "The last Alsatian I had died years ago."

"It's okay," the policeman said, "we won't prosecute you or anything. I'm made up that fella got bitten. We've been after him for months."

Irene still insisted she did not own a dog and the policeman called in a policewoman to make a cup of tea for her as she was still trembling.

About half an hour later, when the police had taken the criminals to the station, the policewoman was having a chat with Irene when they heard a panting noise and the patter of an animal's claws on the tiles of the kitchen. The policewoman went to investigate but the kitchen was empty and in darkness. The WPC shook her head and looked at Irene, who had a bemused look on her face.

"Wasn't that weird?" asked the policewoman. She then left, saying that she would get someone from the social services to pop in the next day to see if she needed any help and that she would send her boyfriend around to fix the broken front door. The time was now ten minutes past four in the morning and Irene was feeling worn out. She put two bolts on the broken door and retired to her bedroom.

At twenty to six that morning, Irene was woken by something wet and cold prodding her hand, which was hanging over the bed. The wet thing was the nose of a big Alsatian dog which was looking at her with brown sorrowful eyes. Irene was shocked at the sight. It was her old dog Bob, who had died fourteen years ago.

Irene reached out to stroke her faithful old friend but, at that moment, the dog vanished. As the pale light of dawn came into the room, Irene felt a tremendous sense of sorrow tinged with disbelief. Until that eventful morning, Irene had not believed in ghosts but now she almost cried as she realised that her dog had somehow returned from the afterlife to protect her.

There is a strange epilogue to this story: when Carla returned from France, she had some film left in her camera from the holiday trip and she took a picture of her mum standing in the garden with her walking stick. When the pictures came back from the chemist, Carla looked at the developed pictures and exclaimed, "Hey mum, look at this. There's a dog on this photo; look, next to you in the garden. I didn't see a dog when I took it."

Irene sighed when she inspected the picture. In the photograph, there was an out of focus image of a big Alsatian sitting behind Irene in the background. The dog was looking at Irene with its head tilted. "That's Bob," Irene whispered, with a lump in her throat. She didn't want to scare Carla, so she didn't mention the apparition of her faithful friend.

"Whose dog is it, mum?" asked Carla.

"I don't know," said her mother, as a tear rolled down her cheek.

Little Arrows

The events in the following bizarre tale allegedly took place in Liverpool in the late summer of 1996. Even seasoned paranormal investigators think the incident is similar to a Disney fairy tale but, unlike a fairy tale, there is physical evidence and the testimony from solicitors and a doctor to suggest that this astounding story is true.

In the August of 1996, a solicitor named Joanne and her estate agent husband Brian, bought a splendid-looking Victorian house situated in Liverpool's Belvidere Road, next to Sefton Park. The professional couple fell in love with the house and its beautiful back garden, both noticing a warm, welcoming atmosphere in the garden which they found difficult to explain.

The couple hired a few experienced decorators who transformed the house into a stylish comfortable home but they faced a problem of what to do with the untamed garden. Joanne wanted an S-shaped path with a greenhouse and a little hut that looked like a miniature black and white Tudor cottage but Brian laughed at the idea, preferring the garden to be practical with an organic herb section, which Joanne thought would look like an allotment. The couple just could not agree.

One warm August evening, as they strolled about the garden, they noticed there was a moss-covered stone about three feet in height, situated in the middle of the garden. It was shaped like an upside down ice-cream cone. Joanne and Brian took a closer look at the stone and saw that there were tiny intricate carvings on it of spirals and little stars. There were also small holes in the stone just big enough to put your finger in. The couple were baffled at the function of the stone, and surmised it was purely ornamental. Joanne thought it was unsightly, but Brian was intrigued by it. Coming from Yorkshire originally, Brian recalled seeing similar stones with identical carvings on the bleak moors to the south of Ilkley. Brian's grandfather had called the stones 'fairy stones' and said they were the homes of the little folk who used to have magical battles with the Druids.

"It's got to go," Joanne insisted. "We can't have a stone in the middle of the garden. It looks like a bollard."

"It's very heavy," Brian groaned, as he tried unsuccessfully to rock the stone. "It'll take some force to uproot it."

"I'm not having it in the middle of my garden; it looks ridiculous," Joanne snapped, walking back into the house.

A few days later, while Brian was at work, Joanne made a few telephone calls. That afternoon, two of her cousins and two old college friends turned up and they dug around the stone. The stone went down into the clay and soil much deeper than Joanne expected, and the shafts of three of the spades snapped as the diggers tried to lever it up. After two hours, the stone finally keeled over at a 45-degree angle but it just could not be uprooted. Joanne congratulated the friends and relatives at their attempts and they all went inside to have a drink and a much deserved rest. Then something bizarre happened. Joanne and her four guests started to sneeze and they could not stop for almost fifteen minutes. At one point, Joanne's cousin started crying as blood poured from her nose. By coincidence, a doctor friend happened to call at the house with a bottle of wine and flowers for the couple. He was intrigued by the outbreak of sneezing and suggested that it was an allergic reaction to the pollen from the disturbed weeds in the back garden.

As he pontificated, Joanne's cat tore into the living room in a frantic state. The cat seemed to be running from something in the garden and was so terrified, it cried out and clawed its way up the new curtains and perched itself on the curtain rail, trembling. When Joanne finally coaxed her cat down, she stroked him and felt the animal's fur. There were sharp objects in the cat's coat. They were tiny little arrows about two inches in length with minute feathers at the end.

Joanne took the cat to the vet and he extracted three more of the tiny arrows from the cat's back leg. The vet said kids with a home-made blowpipe were probably behind the cruel act and the cat was then given a mild sedative to calm its nerves.

On Joanne's return, Brian showed her a tiny note he had found on the dislodged stone. The note was hardly bigger than a postage stamp and under a magnifying glass, there was a tiny message scrawled 'Put the stone back or die'. Joanne thought Brian had written the little note and told him to grow up but Brian insisted he had not written it, having thought that she or her friends had.

Later that evening, Brian and Joanne got into their new Vauxhall Corsa to go to a friend's house but the car refused to start. Joanne remarked "Someone's put the evil eye on us." As she walked back to the front door of the house, intending to phone for a taxi, something hit her on the head. It was an egg, a free range egg that had gone missing from the fridge earlier that day. This really spooked Joanne and Brian and having cancelled their night out, they walked into the garden to survey the dislodged stone.

"If I wasn't a level-headed person, I'd say this thing is the source of all these weird incidents," Brian said, eying the small leaning megalith.

"You're giving me the creeps. Shut up!" exclaimed Joanne and she pulled her husband up the path, back to the house. Then she cried out and clutched at her right ear, running into the house crying with pain. When Brian examined Joanne's ear, he saw a tiny little arrow in it. The tip of the sinister little missile seemed to be stuck inside the ear near to the eardrum. Brian got a pair of tweezers out of the first aid kit and plucked out the arrow. It was identical to the little arrows that had been shot into Joanne's cat.

Throughout the remainder of that night, things kept hitting the couple's bedroom window every few minutes. Joanne got Brian to draw the curtains and the couple embraced each other anxiously until daybreak. Throughout the night, Joanne's cat screeched as if something was tormenting it. Next day, Brian got as many friends as he could muster and, without telling them why, he got them to put the dislodged stone in the garden back into its upright position. After that was done, an uneasy silence descended on the house in Belvidere Road for three days. Then Brian found another tiny note on the step of the back door. The tiny word on it simply said, 'Thanks'.

The garden is now an abandoned wilderness with weeds running rampant and shabby-looking thistles flourishing were roses should be in bloom, because Brian and Joanne refuse to venture there in case the phantom archers take aim again. Even the many paranormal investigators who have investigated the case will not be associated with it because the incident seems so unbelievable. However, the first Anglo-Saxon settlers in England mentioned being fired upon by so-called 'elf shot', tiny arrows aimed at them by the little spirit folk who were said to be the original inhabitants of the British Isles.

The Hitch-hiker

The following incident allegedly happened in Liverpool in 1979 and was even mentioned in a local TV news programme.

In the autumn of 1979, a man named Frank Haines was driving his Ford Cortina along Queens Drive near Dunbabin Road in the Wavertree district of the city. The time was 1.45am, and it was raining heavily. Frank had been to visit his old mother in the Dingle and was on his way home. However, his Cortina had a troublesome engine and whenever Frank stopped at the lights, the car would stall or shudder.

On this particular, rainy night, the car pulled up at the traffic lights and the engine died. Frank had to turn the ignition key again and again to get the car to start. Seconds before he was going to move off, a girl came running through the torrential rain, waving at him through the rain-lashed windscreen. She ran up to the Cortina and tapped on the passenger window. Frank saw that the girl looked as if she was about 19 or 20 years of age. She wore a white rain-soaked tee shirt, a tartan scarf, and a pair of white flares. He leaned over and opened the door and the girl climbed in the car, slammed the door and sat in the seat wiping the rain from her face. She had long red hair and a pale freckled face.

"Could you give me a lift home, mate?" she asked, smiling at Frank.

"Do you always jump in strangers' cars like that?" said Frank, annoyed because the engine was refusing to start. As he turned the ignition key once more, the engine fired into life. "Where do you want a lift to?" he asked the girl.

"Barnham Drive, please," the girl replied and gave the number of her house.

"Where's that?" Frank asked, relieved that the car was moving along once again.

"It's off Childwall Valley Road," said the girl and she leaned back, let out a sigh and started singing a song Frank had not heard for years. It was a Bay City Rollers song 'Bye Bye Baby'.

"What are you doing out at this time?" Frank asked the girl.

"I've been walking for the last half an hour from Fir Lane through this rain. I hate the rain, don't you?" the girl replied. Then she asked, "What's your name?"

"Frank. What's yours?" Frank accelerated through a set of traffic lights that were about to turn red to avoid stalling again.

"Kelly."

"Well, Kelly, you'll have to direct me to Barnham Drive."

Frank drove to the Fiveways roundabout and carried on along Childwall Valley Road.

"Thanks for the lift, Frank. Are you going out your way for me?" said Kelly, beaming a smile at the driver.

"Nah, I'm not going out of the way; I live over in Court Hey. Now. Where do I go now?" said Frank, squinting at the road through the squeaking windscreen wipers.

"It's on your right here – no, its the next road on the right," said Kelly. Then she tapped Frank on his left leg.

"What?" said Frank, startled.

"Frank, could you do me a favour? But you'll think I'm cheeky." asked Kelly. "Could you wait outside the house for me, then give me a lift to my mate in Chelwood Avenue? Could you?"

"Look, I'm not a bloody taxi driver. I'm dropping you off at your house and that's it," Frank retorted as he turned into Barnham Drive and stopped near the girl's house.

"Please, Frank? The girl touched Frank's knee and playfully pinched it, making him smile. "Pretty please?"

"Hurry up then. You've got five minutes. If this car doesn't start though, I'll have to walk home." Frank shook his head.

"Thanks, Frank. I won't be a minute. I'll just tell my Dad I'm staying over at my mate's." Kelly left the car and dashed down the road in the pouring rain. She opened her gate and disappeared behind a hedge as she ran up the path towards the door.

Frank was thirty-three, but looked much younger. He wondered if he was too old to date Kelly. She only looked about 20. He dismissed the thought from his mind and waited for her to come back. He waited … and waited. Fifteen minutes crawled by and Frank started to get annoyed. "That's it, girl; I'm going home," he muttered. He decided to just give Kelly another five minutes but the girl still did not return. Frank surmised that her father had told her she could not get into a car with a stranger. Frank started the car up first time and began to drive off but, a few seconds later, the car started to shake and shuddered to a halt. Frank tried again and again to get it to restart but it just would not budge. He cursed Kelly and thought, "Damn it! She imposed on me, now I will ask her for help." Frank marched to Kelly's house and rang the bell. He knew deep down that it was also a good excuse to see Kelly again. She was a very pretty girl and Frank recalled the way she touched his leg in the car. A silhouette came and looked through the frosted glass. "Who is it?" said a voice behind the door.

"It's me; Frank. Is Kelly there?"

A bolt was drawn back behind the door and the handle turned. The front door opened and a man aged about sixty peered out at Frank.

"Sorry to bother you. Is Kelly there?" Frank asked, dripping wet and burning with embarrassment.

"Kelly who?" the man demanded. Frank noticed that the man held an Alsatian dog by the collar with the other hand.

Frank told the man about the red-haired girl he'd given a lift to and the man seemed flabbergasted and badly shaken.

The man said his daughter Kelly had been knocked down in a hit and run incident on Fir Lane four years ago. He was so shaken by the story, he invited Frank in out of the rain and showed Frank his photo album of Kelly. In one photograph, she was dressed in the tartan and white flares that Bay City Rollers fans wore and Frank remembered the song she had sung in his car – 'Bye Bye Baby'. Just before Kelly died, her friend in Court Hey had had an argument with her and cried her eyes out when she heard that Kelly had died. She kept saying she wished she could say she was sorry to Kelly.

It is said that Kelly's ghost still walks up Fir Lane and has even been seen by the police. In 1990, it was reported that a Royal Mail van had swerved to avoid the ghost of a red-haired girl who vanished in the middle of the road.

Ghostly Visions

Throughout the history of the human race, people have reported seeing strange visions; whether they are images of strange ships in the sky or an apparition of the Virgin Mary, they are usually defined as hallucinations. The following two stories are about strange visions that have been seen by people in the north west region.

In the early 1950s, a Welsh tugboat was cruising through the sea, about 15 miles north of the Great Orme's Head off Llandudno. The sun had just gone down when the skipper of the tug was intrigued to see a group of objects bobbing about in the waters about a quarter of a mile away. He looked at the objects through his old telescope and was startled to see that they were the heads of about five or six men in the water. The skipper steered his tug to the scene and surmised that the men had fallen from a capsized lifeboat. Upon reaching the spot, he saw that there was nobody in the water. He killed the engine of the tugboat and listened until the silence became unnerving.

Later that night, the skipper informed a fellow mariner at Liverpool Docks about the strange faces in the waves, and he was told that he had seen the ghosts of the men who had perished in that exact spot off Llandudno in 1939 when their submarine, *Thetis*, sank during her trials. The submarine had dived and got her nose stuck in the thick mud and silt on the seabed. Although the tail of the submarine was sticking out of the waters, the unfortunate captain and crew could not be saved. All would-be rescuers were warned off by the Admiralty, because the submarine was top secret. No one was allowed to damage it by cutting an escape hole in its hull. There were only four survivors who escaped by firing themselves out of the torpedo tubes. The rest died slowly from oxygen starvation and could be heard tapping frantically on the hull. It is said that the faces of the doomed submariners still appear in the waves above the wreck of the sub, which lies on the bed of the sea off the north coast of Wales.

Another vision which is hard to explain occurred in the home of an old spinster named Gwen Mallory, who lived in a crumbling old house in Mulgrave Street in Toxteth. The year was 1837 and, one freezing January night, sixty-seven-year-old Miss Mallory and her beautiful 15 year-old niece, Alice, gathered around the blazing coal fire. Alice was stabbing the glowing coals with the poker when her old Auntie Gwen suddenly grabbed the girl's hand and told her to stop poking the fire because she could see pictures in the flames. Alice was fascinated by her aunt's remark and asked her what she could see. Miss Mallory said, "I see a girl on the throne of our kingdom. A plain-looking girl. She will become queen after our king dies."

Alice became excited, then screamed as her aunty fell forward toward the fire as if she was in a deep trance. The teenager caught her in time, and the old spinster came to her senses. Later that year, in June, King William IV died, and a plain-looking girl did become the Queen; she was, of course, Queen Victoria.

The old spinster of Mulgrave Street saw many more strange visions in the flames, and her niece noted them all down in a book which disappeared at the turn of the 19th century. All we have today are the stories and rumours of the recorded predictions. It was said that Mallory foresaw the Liverpool Blitz in the incandescent coals of her grate, and described the Luftwaffe as "a gathering of black iron eagles which would drop fire and death on the town". She also made an intriguing reference to a future cultural revolution and it is known to be genuine, because a sceptical writer named Charles Mann wrote in 1870 that Miss Mallory prophesied that 'a band of minstrels would set the world dancing to the beat of their drum in the next century, which will be a time of great change and never-ending strife.' Many occultists have surmised that the minstrels were the Beatles and the time of change and strife was the 1960s, the decade which saw riots in the United States, the assassinations of President Kennedy, his brother Robert and Martin Luther King, the Vietnam War, the Moon Landings and many other historical turning points.

Unlike the other prophets, such as Nostradamus, the Seeress of Mulgrave Street saw a golden future for mankind prophesying, "One day all the nations will put their differences aside and unite under a blue and white banner." She also mentioned the arrival of a "great teacher who will come down from a mountain."

Noisy Neighbours

The Bullring is a row of tenements off Brownlow Hill, so-called because of the circular layout of the dwellings. In 1972, at a flat in these tenements, a very strange paranormal incident occurred that was witnessed by four people, including two policemen.

A young couple, Julie and Frank, moved into a flat on the top floor of the Bullring in the summer of 1972. Julie was a barmaid at a local pub, the Oxford, and Frank worked at a bakery in Toxteth. One night, at around 11 o'clock, Frank returned home from the bakery and saw that Julie was not yet home. He was about to make himself a TV dinner and listen to some music when he heard a terrible noise next door. Frank shook his head and said, "Noisy neighbours. That's all I need right now."

And the noise got steadily worse. Frank heard the man next door shout, "You idiot! You've really done it now!"

Then a woman's hysterical voice screamed, "I'm sorry, Keith!" Followed by the sound of objects being thrown about and plates being smashed.

Frank thumped on the wall and shouted "Oi! That's enough! Shut up!"

The noise subsided but, half an hour later, when Frank was settling down to eat his supper, the arguers started again. Frank shook his head and listened to the neighbours squabbling.

"I can't believe what you've done. That's it, you're dead now, girl, you're dead!" shouted the man.

"No, you're dead now! I mean it!" she screamed back.

Frank then heard plates being smashed. There was a knock at the door and he got up, accidentally dropping the plate with his supper onto the sofa. He was fuming as he answered the door to let Julie in. She had returned home from work and told him two policemen were on the landing outside, hammering on the door of the flat next door because there was a domestic incident taking place. Frank said, "Tell me about it. They're at each other's throats."

The screams next door got louder, so the policemen had no choice but to kick the door in. Inside, they found no one, just fragments of crockery in the kitchen and smashed ornaments in the living room. This obviously unnerved the policemen and they looked out of the window in case the battling couple had jumped or pushed each other to the street below, but they had not.

Three hours later, it was discovered that the couple next door could not have been having a heated argument because they had died earlier in the evening in a car crash over a mile away in Princes Road. The woman, who had been driving, had been drinking before the journey and had hit a lamppost at 50 mph, killing herself and her husband instantly.

When a relative of the dead couple turned up at the flat and later spoke to Frank and Julie next door about the tragedy, Frank's blood ran cold as he remembered what he had heard the man next door saying: "I can't believe what you've done. That's it, you're dead now!" he had said and she had replied to him "No, you're dead." It suddenly made sense to Frank. He had heard two ghosts fighting next door; the two spirits of the crash victims had come home, arguing over who was to blame for their deaths. Understandably, Julie and Frank left their flat that same week.

Tales of Christmas Past

Ever since Marley's ghost appeared to Scrooge in Dickens's *A Christmas Carol*, back in 1843, the Season of Goodwill has become a traditional time for telling ghost stories. What better time to settle down in the hearthside glow of a fire to listen to a spooky story or spine-tingling tale before retiring to bed? Here are three local supernatural tales which took place around Yuletide. The first story is from the 20th century and the other two tales are from the Victorian period. One of these Christmas tales, *Note to Santa*, was broadcast on local radio in 1997, narrated by velvet-voiced DJ Terry Lennaine and resulted in an avalanche of letters from people wanting to hear the seasonal tale again. A 15-stone bouncer even wrote to the *Liverpool Echo*, confessing that he had unashamedly cried upon hearing the tale! Anyway, here's the first story. Have a hanky ready.

In 1990 in Merseyside, a childless couple jumped at the opportunity of fostering Gary, an 11-year-old boy. The authorities told the couple that Gary had been put up for adoption twice before but had been returned to the care of the social services for being unusually hyperactive. The couple took Gary home a fortnight before Christmas and totally spoiled him. The child excitedly said he wanted three Christmas stockings, and was given them. The couple put up a huge tree and laid bundles of presents for Gary under it. The child opened some of these presents but the couple did not scold him, they just laughed about it and allowed the boy to take the gifts – a box of antique tin soldiers and a little drum up to his room.

At 3.00am the couple were awakened by the sound of a strange racket which was coming from Gary's bedroom. The foster-parents jumped out of bed and barged into Gary's room and were shocked at the bizarre sight which greeted them. The drum was beating all by itself and all the little tin soldiers were hopping along the floor in a single file to the drumbeat. A sleepy-eyed Gary was sitting up in his bed, giggling and clapping his hands as he surveyed the eerie spectacle. The couple, who were very religious, took the poltergeist-like phenomenon as a manifestation of the Devil and promptly decided they did not want to adopt the child. During the journey to the social services department, strange knocking sounds were heard on the side windows of the couple's car. Once again, Gary spent his Christmas without a mum and dad, because he probably possessed the psychic gift of telekinesis: the ability to move objects by the power of the mind. The problem child's fate is unknown.

The Christmas Spectre

There is a certain old house in Liverpool's Clarence Street that is the scene of supernatural unrest every time the festive season is upon us. Strange rappings are heard on doors and the sounds of a disgruntled voice cursing a long-dead man named Charles reach their highest around Christmas Eve, when the ruffled ghost appears. He is a man of around 50 years of age who wears a long purple velveteen coat, a grey waistcoat, and a pair of long narrow trousers. Many people have seen him over the years, from the late 19th century to the present day. From the accounts given by terrified witnesses, we know that the Christmas spectre of Clarence Street smokes an ectoplasmic pipe and wears a pair of wire-framed spectacles, which he peers over as he paces backwards and forwards before a cast-iron fireplace in the sitting room of the house. The phantom goes through his paces in his personal limbo at the same time every Christmas Eve, at precisely ten to eleven at night. The spectre always ends his ghostly performance by resting his head on the mantelpiece and sobbing. He then fades away, leaving an aromatic mist of pipe tobacco hanging in the air.

Five years ago, the ghost put in his seasonal appearance and the poor tomcat of the family who were staying there was so terrified it leapt out the first floor window and almost ended life number nine.

For years, generations of residents at the haunted house have pondered on the ghost's identity, but a couple of years ago, a certain professional ghost researcher and two local historians finally solved the mystery of this ghost of Christmas past. Here's the tale they uncovered.

At the aforementioned address in Clarence Street, there lived a middle-aged bachelor, a doctor named Humphrey Brooke, who became infatuated with a girl less than half his age. She was the daughter of a Duke Street shipping magnate and was named Felicia

Clayton. Felicia was 20 years old with flaxen blonde hair and a stunning, curvaceous figure. Many men were in love with the girl and she was constantly receiving invitations to every ball and soiree in the city. Humphrey Brooke was around 50 years of age and knew that he would never be regarded as attractive by the opposite sex. He had a hook nose, failing eyesight, a stoop from hunching over his medical books and an asthmatic cough because of his incessant pipe-smoking. On top of all of that, he suffered from long bouts of debilitating rheumatism in his joints. Yet, he was completely infatuated with the seemingly untouchable Felicia.

It all started in the autumn of that year when Brooke attended the funeral of Jesse Hartley, the eminent engineer who had transformed the Liverpool waterfront with his magnificent docks and warehouses. Felicia and her father attended the funeral too, and Dr Brooke was briefly introduced to the young beauty. He kissed her hand and she smiled at him several times during that sombre afternoon. Since then, he had only seen Miss Clayton twice. Once in Rodney Street, alighting from a hansom cab and, on the second occasion, she had waved to the doctor in Bold Street while walking hand in hand with a rich suitor, a young Colonel Burns. Dr Brooke was flabbergasted at the way Felicia had charmingly acknowledged him with that wave of her gloved hand. The girl and her beau walked on down Bold Street but she turned twice and smiled at Dr Brooke and this naturally turned the Colonel crimson with jealousy.

The bachelor Brooke returned to his house with a spring in his step and wrote of his encounters with Felicia in a little black book. Brooke also scribbled down his outrageous plans to win Felicia's heart. The most realistic plan was quite straightforward. A Christmas Eve ball was to take place at the prestigious address of a Rodney Street magistrate. Humphrey Brooke had already received an invitation to the ball. The invitation card said the doctor was entitled to bring a lady friend to the ball so Mr Brooke lovingly wrote the name Felicia Clayton on the invite and studied how the ornate card looked with his name next to the woman who was the light of his life in those short, gloomy December days.

The following morning, Dr Brooke's friend, Charles Wilson, the proprietor of a corn mill, visited his friend at the surgery in Clarence Street. Wilson was five years younger than his doctor friend, and enjoyed a legendary reputation for being a womaniser. Wilson asked Brooke if he had anything planned for Christmas and asked him if he wanted a bit of company in the taverns of Liverpool over the festive season. Dr Brooke said he had plans for Christmas Eve which involved a beautiful young woman. Wilson said, "This isn't another of your fantasies involving a certain Miss Clayton, who is young enough to be your daughter, is it?"

Before he could answer, a woman rushed into the surgery and pleaded with Dr Brooke to come at once to treat her father, who had collapsed and was having a seizure. Brooke knew the woman's father well so he grabbed his medical bag and rushed out the surgery, leaving Wilson behind. Wilson was a nosey fellow and he opened a drawer in the doctor's desk and read the little black book. Wilson grinned and sniggered as he read the book's entries about Felicia.

"Ah, there's no fool like an old fool," Wilson whispered to himself as he noticed the invitation card with his friend's name on, and Felicia's name next to it.

Wilson was intrigued at his friend's crush on the sensuous, young woman and he paid a visit to Dr Brooke the following afternoon. Wilson chuckled and asked the doctor if Felicia had accepted his invitation. Brooke was outraged and realised that Wilson had read his secret journal. "How dare you pry into my personal life?" Brooke reprimanded Wilson. But the lovelorn doctor had a surprise for his nosey friend. He produced a letter and handed it to him.

"What's this? A writ for prying?" Wilson joked but when he read the letter, its contents wiped the smile off his face. It was from Felicia Clayton. She had accepted Dr Brooke's invitation to the Christmas Eve dance ball. Wilson was instantly consumed with jealousy. He threw the letter on the desk and left, saying, "Ha! It will all come to nothing. Age and youth are like oil and water, they can never mix."

That Christmas Eve, Doctor Brooke wore a fine purple velveteen jacket and his best embroidered grey silken waistcoat. He stood before the fireplace, pacing up and down, with butterflies in his stomach, a feeling he had not experienced since the courting days of his youth, so many years ago. There was a heavy jangling of the front door bell which startled the doctor. He answered, thinking that perhaps Felicia had decided to call upon him, but the caller was a shivering red-nosed youth; a messenger boy who handed Dr Brooke a sealed envelope. Brooke tipped the messenger and read the letter. His heart broke on the spot. Felicia had undergone a dramatic change of heart and no longer wished to go to the dance with the doctor. She was now going to the ball with her long-time admirer Colonel Burns. The letter, written by Felicia's stern father, warned Brooke to keep away from his daughter in future and to act his age. Unknown to Brooke, his so-called friend Charles Wilson had sent an anonymous letter to Felicia's father, warning him of Dr Brooke's 'outrageous and obnoxious plans to have romantic involvements' with Felicia.

Felicia, however, was a strong-headed girl and disobeyed her father's instructions by going to the Christmas Eve ball, where she looked everywhere for Dr Brooke. Felicia knew the doctor was not much to look at, but his romantic letters to her had moved her, and Felicia had been determined to meet Humphrey. When the doctor failed to turn up, Felicia went home, much to the disappointment of all the men at the ball.

Doctor Brooke was devastated by the letter and, on that Christmas Eve, he died from what seems to have been a heart attack, brought on by the emotional turmoil of the apparent rejection from Felicia. Brooke knocked the clock from the mantelpiece as he fell dead on the hearth rug, and the clock broke; its dial recorded that the death had occurred at precisely ten to eleven. And that's the sad history of the Christmas spectre.

Note to Santa

The following story is a true tale which took place long ago on a bitterly cold Christmas Eve of 1868 in the Edge Hill district of Liverpool. The snow was fluttering down on a little run-down house in Oxford Street East while, outside, a choir sang Silent Night.

When the choir called at number 52 Oxford Street East at 7.00pm, a woman with a sad, ashen face and heavy, sorrowful eyes answered. Her seven-year-old daughter, Annie, came from behind her mother clutching an old worn-out and patched-up doll. Little Annie smiled at the choir. She could hardly see them because she was partially sighted, but she imagined the singers as a flock of angels. When the choir stopped singing, Annie's mother, Kate, could only offer them a few farthings. A small boy held out his cap and received the coins with a grateful bow, saying, "God bless you ma'am. A merry Christmas to you and your family."

Kate smiled and nodded, then closed the door. Behind the door, she stood there, trying not to cry. Little Annie held onto her mum's dress and said, "Mummy don't be sad. Please don't cry, Dolly doesn't like it when you cry." Annie held up the little threadbare doll and shook it.

Kate stooped down and hugged her little daughter and said, "Oh, I love you, little Annie. You're the most beautiful little girl in the world."

The past year had been like a nightmare. Kate's husband, a coalman, had died of cholera and left her a widow at 27 years of age. Only the love of her little daughter had kept her going but, each day, life seemed to get harder. Kate was now living in a rundown dwelling owned by an elderly, cold-hearted landlord named John Stanley. Mr Stanley had warned Kate that if she did not pay off her rent arrears soon she would be thrown out, along with her daughter. Mr Stanley had called earlier in the day but Kate had been out with Annie buying the food rations for that week; a little Christmas pudding, a loaf, two mince pies, a couple of oranges and a small slice of mouldy-looking cheese. Mr Stanley had left a note on the mantelpiece saying he would be back later and expected to be paid. Kate thought about bolting the door to the callous Mr Stanley but Mr Stanley had been barred from entering his premises by previous tenants and had long removed the bolts from the doors of the dwelling.

Kate undressed Annie in front of the fire and told her not to expect anything from Father Christmas because Santa had told her he was very busy this year but he had promised to bring presents to Annie in the New Year. "Oh," was all that Annie could utter and she bowed her head slightly and a little tear trickled from her eye. Annie quickly wiped it away and put on a brave smile. She said, "I don't need any presents because I've got dolly."

Kate hugged her daughter then lit a candle and led her up to her bedroom. As she was tucking Annie into the bed, she noticed a folded piece of brown parcel paper sticking out from under Annie's pillow. Kate retrieved the scrap of paper and hid it in her hand. She then kissed her daughter and said, "Goodnight Annie, goodnight dolly.

Sleep tight."

Downstairs by the light of the fire and the flickering candle, Kate's heart broke when she saw what was written on the piece of paper. In enormous childish letters, the visually disadvantaged child had tried to write out a list of things she wanted from Father Christmas. Kate held her head in her hands and quietly sobbed. She felt so hopeless and alone. A little mouse warming itself near the fire was the only company Kate had. Suddenly she heard the rattle of the key in the lock. It was Mr Stanley, the hard-hearted landlord. "So, you're finally in, eh?" he snorted as he entered the room.

Kate sniffled and nodded as the mouse ran off into the darkness.

"You owe me ten shillings in arrears. I want it now," demanded the landlord holding out his hand.

"I don't have the money, Mr Stanley," Kate said, with a tremor in her voice.

Mr Stanley picked up the poker and walked about the room, grumbling to himself. "You're out of here first thing in the morning. And I don't care if it is Christmas, I'm sick of tenants taking liberties with me."

"But I've nowhere to go. And what about my child?" Kate pleaded, expecting Mr Stanley to show some humanity in the Season of Goodwill.

"That is your problem. Pay up now or get out," the landlord snapped as he hurled the poker into the grate, startling the widow.

"Would you accept my husband's silver pocket watch? That's all I have," said Kate, in desperation. The watch was of great sentimental value but the wellbeing of Annie and herself had to come first in these hard times.

"It all depends on its condition," said Mr Stanley in a grumpy voice.

Kate hurried up to her room to get the pocket watch. When she came back downstairs a minute later, the landlord was not around. "Mr Stanley?" Kate shouted, but there was no reply. She went outside, and caught a glimpse of Mr Stanley hurrying down the street. He was barely visible as he rushed into the raging blizzard that had suddenly descended on the town. Kate was puzzled and went back into the house.

Something strange happened in the early hours of that Christmas morn. Little Annie was awakened by something. Her eyesight was not good enough to see who was standing in her room but it seemed to be a figure carrying a sack. Who else could he be? Annie smiled, "Is that you Mr Christmas?" She felt so sleepy, and thought it was all a dream.

The figure whispered, "Sshhh! Little angel. Go to sleep or you'll find ashes on your bed in the morning."

Annie squeezed an eye shut and watched the fuzzy figure move out the room and heard him creeping down the stairs. She decided it was all a dream and went back to sleep.

On Christmas morning, Kate awoke and found a box and a parcel at her bedside. The gifts were wrapped in expensive paper and tied up with golden, silk ribbons. A card on one gift bore the message, 'A Merry Christmas to you, my dear'. Kate hurried downstairs, expecting to find someone in the house who had perpetrated this prank. There was no one about and who would go to such lengths to play such a joke? Kate was completely baffled. She opened the parcel and saw it was a beautiful long velveteen dress. The box contained a stylish, expensive bonnet. Then the mystery deepened. In the kitchen, she found someone had left a hamper, crammed with food. It contained a turkey wrapped in a muslin cloth and a huge family-sized Christmas pudding. Among the rest of the contents there was a bottle of Exshaw's four-star brandy. Kate thought she was dreaming and went upstairs to wish her daughter a Merry Christmas and to tell her of the food left by the phantom Samaritan. Then Kate got the shock of her life. Entering the bedroom, there was little Annie, fast asleep among a clutter of wrapped presents. Boxes of every size, large and small littered the child's bed and the floor of the room. Kate clasped her hands together and said, "Oh thank you, sweet Jesus."

She woke Annie, and the little girl was naturally completely overwhelmed by the presents from the mysterious benefactor. The brightly-coloured parcels contained costly porcelain dolls, a large house for them to live in, a musical jewellery box, a pretty little bonnet that fitted Annie perfectly, a little pram, and a beautiful royal blue dress trimmed with fine lace. However, there were no cards to indicate who had left the child's gifts. Annie excitedly told her mother about the man in her room with the sack who had told her to sleep but she could not give a description because of her partial blindness. She merely added that the man had a kind voice and must have been Father Christmas.

Sometime later, Kate noticed that the little note that Annie had written to Santa had vanished from the mantelpiece. Stranger still, the landlord never bothered her again. He never came back to demand his rent. Five years later, Kate's luck suddenly changed. A cousin died and left her a substantial amount of money in his will. Kate and her daughter left the dwelling in Oxford Street East and, on the day they were leaving, Kate and her daughter called upon the landlord to hand in the keys. Kate asked Mr Stanley why he had never taken rent since that Christmas Eve. The old landlord seemed reluctant to reply initially and seemed all choked up with emotion. Then he told a sad tale.

One Christmas Eve, when he was thirty, he was returning to his home with a sack of the presents for his daughter and wife. To his horror, when he arrived he discovered that his six-year-old daughter, Emily, and wife, Lydia, had died in a tragic blaze which had gutted his home. Mr Stanley was naturally devastated and, when the fire had died down, he searched in the burnt-out shell which once had been his happy family home. As the snow fell upon the charred remains of what had been little Emily's bedroom, Mr Stanley found a sock Emily had hung on the foot of her bed, along with a scrap of paper. It had been Emily's note to Santa, listing all the presents she wanted.

Mr Stanley broke down upon finding that little piece of paper and carried it about with him for the rest of his life. The loss of his wife and daughter made the landlord an embittered man and people mistook his bitterness for coldheartedness. So, that Christmas Evening, when he had gone to Kate's dwelling, demanding his rent, he had noticed little Annie's note to Santa on the mantelpiece while Kate was upstairs fetching her late husband's pocket watch. The little note to Santa had been too much for the landlord to bear and he left in tears brought on by so many painful memories. It also made John Stanley have a dramatic change of heart. He returned to Kate's house and let himself in with his key carrying the sack of presents originally intended for his wife and daughter. He had been Santa to little Annie and her poor mother.

The Devil's Children

The following chilling story took place in the North-West in November, 1858. Isaac West, a writer from Wolverhampton, was travelling around the country collecting folk tales for a book. He was determined to spend many years visiting every corner of Britain to record all the tales and myths of the land. The writer didn't believe in ghosts or the world of the supernatural and thought that the Devil was just a figment of the human imagination.

On this particular foggy evening, West mounted his horse and rode from a country inn on the outskirts of Ormskirk towards a lodging house near the town of Rufford, just five miles to the north. During the journey he noticed a rosy glow in the forest to his left. Curiosity got the better of the writer and he dismounted, tethered the reins of his horse to a tree and set off towards the light. As he drew nearer he realised that it was a bonfire.

There were around 30 strange, robed figures standing in a circle around the bonfire, and they all wore pointed white hats with eye-holes in. This was ten years before the Ku Klux Klan was founded but the costume the figures wore looked just like the garments and hats which were later worn by the members of the racist secret society in America.

As he crept closer to get a better view, West saw something that sent a shudder down his spine. One of the figures took a crying baby from a box and walked over to the fire while the other figures chanted something. West noticed that there was an enormous wooden cross with a man crucified upon it above the raging flames. It was a real body on the cross and not an effigy. The cross was turned upside down and so was the figure on it. The bonfire had been built around this horrific crucifixion and the man on the cross looked dead and burnt to charcoal. The figure cradling the child in its arms moved even nearer to the fire. West was horrified. It seemed as if the figure was about to throw the baby onto the flames. He knew it was madness but something inside West impelled him to try and save the baby. Snapping off a large leafless branch of a tree, he saw to his horror that the figure was now holding the baby up to the burnt man on the upside-down cross.

West rushed out of hiding and ran up to the figure holding the baby, whacking him hard on the back of the head with the heavy branch. The other startled figures turned and watched as he grabbed the baby from the masked sadist and run back into the forest.

Isaac West felt as if he was experiencing a terrible nightmare as he ran through the forest with the little baby in his arms. He could hear the masked figures chasing after him. He felt a stabbing stitch of pain in his side but kept running. He realised that he had lost track of where he had tied his horse because of the fog and this naturally made him panic for his life, because he knew those people in close pursuit were Devil worshippers and they would think nothing of killing the writer to silence him.

The outline of his horse appeared out of the fog and West raced towards it but, as he did so, a rifle shot whistled past his head and the horse whinnied pitifully and fell down. West kept running although he felt his lungs were going to explode. He thought about dropping the child and running off to save his own life but just could not bring himself to commit such a cowardly act. Running out of the forest, he prayed for God to intervene, when the lamps of a stagecoach appeared further down the road towards the village of Parbold. As the clatter of the coach horses drew nearer, West ran into the road and attempted to flag the coach down. He waved at the coach driver, and turned to see the hooded figures watching from the forest. They seemed reluctant to come out of the woodland but watched keenly from the shadows.

The coach pulled up and West fell to his knees with exhaustion, still clutching the crying baby.

"What in damnation is going on?" asked a distinguished voice inside the coach. Isaac West instantly recognised the rich deep voice. It was Horace Jones, a rich industrialist and patron to the arts. West knew him well. He had been a dinner guest of Horace and his Mawdesley-born wife at their magnificent mansion near Nantwich on many occasions over the years. Just what Horace was doing so far north at the dead of night was a mystery but West was so relieved to hear the wealthy man's voice that he gave it little thought.

Horace looked out of the window and squinted at the writer holding the baby. "Is that you Isaac?"

"Horace!" gasped West, pointing to the forest and explaining what he had seen. The magnate seemed very nervous about what he was hearing and, as West made a grab for the doorhandle of the coach, shouted, "No! Stay there! Wait a moment!"

West said the baby was going to die of pneumonia in the chilly night air and, pulling open the carriage door, noticed that Horace was trying to take off the same weird robe that the Devil worshippers were wearing in the forest. On the seat next to Horace Jones was a pointed hat with the eye holes, just like the ones the Devil worshippers were wearing. West was naturally stunned. The industrialist reached into his inside pocket but West dived at him, punching him in the face and making his nose bleed. He then grabbed a small pistol from Horace's inside jacket pocket and held it against his forehead. "Tell the coachman to take us from this accursed place ,or I'll not hesitate to blow your brains out!" demanded West.

Horace was petrified of the mad look in West's eyes and screamed to the coachman, "Do as he says! Hurry!"

As the coach trundled along towards the village of Shevington, Horace claimed that he had been going to attend the sacrifice in the woods to infiltrate and spy upon the satanists. However, West did not believe him and questioned him about who they had taken the infant from. Horace said it was probably from some girl who was herself a satanist.

The baby was left with the landlord of a tavern in Shevington and West reported Horace to the police sheriff in the village. But Horace was rich and powerful and quickly bought himself out of his unsavoury predicament. He claimed that West had an over-imaginative mind but when West and several policemen visited the spot in the forest, they all saw the remains of the bonfire and the blackened upside-down cross. It was determined that the body on that cross was not alive when it had been cremated. The body was athecorpse of a man who had been dug up from the local cemetery before being nailed to the cross. Despite the evidence – including the remains of his horse, West was strongly advised, by certain people in high-ranking positions whom he could not name, to leave the area and go back to Wolverhampton.

It later came to light that there was a satanic cult calling themselves "The Devil's Children" at work in the area committing rape and murder.

When the Ninja Struck in Liverpool

We have all seen the legendary Japanese Ninja warriors in action in films and on TV, but, believe it or not, there was a gruesome murder case in Liverpool in the 1930s, and the killers were thought to have been two Ninjas.

Back Bedford Street South is a narrow, dimly-lit alleyway that runs behind the Cambridge public house. One foggy night at 11.15pm in 1937, a policeman was patrolling Mulberry Street and decided to enjoy a cigarette. He looked about and, seeing there was no one around, lit a Woodbine and stood in the shadows at the top of Back Bedford Street South.

About five minutes later, a figure emerged out of the fog, walking towards him with a hurried gait. As the stranger got nearer, the policeman flicked his cigarette to the floor and turned to the man and put his hand on the handle of his truncheon. The stranger was about five foot three inches in height and of Far Eastern appearance. He bowed his head as he passed the policeman and darted down Back Bedford Street South.

The policeman decided to have another cigarette, as he had not been able to finish the other one in peace. As he struck a match to light up, the officer of the law thought he felt something brush past him, but when he turned around he saw no one was there.

Three minutes later he heard a loud crack echo down the alleyway. Drawing his truncheon, he crept down the alleyway. It was so dark, he had to switch on his bulls' eye torch. The beam of the torch revealed a truly horrific sight. The oriental man who had passed him earlier was sitting up against the wall of the alleyway with a small-handled hatchet buried in his skull. The blow from the killer had been so savage, it had divided the man's head into two equal halves, right down to the neck. As the horrified policeman looked on, blood started to stream down the man's neck and shoulders and, as it did so, the two halves of his head fell further apart. This obviously meant that the killer had struck less than a minute ago.

The policeman put his whistle to his mouth and tried to blow hard but he was so numb with terror the whistle barely produced a peep.

Six feet from the slaughtered victim lay a small black tube with a wisp of smoke rising from it. It looked like some sort of firecracker.

A subsequent investigation deepened the murder mystery. A single Japanese glyph was engraved on the handle of the hatchet and an expert on Far Eastern culture said the Japanese letter referred to some ancient Ninja sect and stood for 'revenge'. Detectives thought it might have been the work of the Chinese Tong but all investigations and enquiries around Chinatown were met with a wall of silence.

Just as the investigation was about to be closed, a woman visited the local police station and told detectives that she had witnessed the murder near Cambridge Street. On the night of the murder, the woman had been about to retire and had casually glanced out of the window before drawing her curtains. Her window was situated opposite the scene of the crime and she had seen a masked man in black creeping behind the policeman, who was having a smoke at the top of the alleyway. This masked figure was incredibly agile, said the woman. He climbed up a pipe just four or five feet behind the policeman and tiptoed along the gutter of the roof that ran down Back Bedford Street South. The masked man then slid down another pipe and in one swift silent movement, he dropped down on his victim and whacked him once on the head with something that looked like a hatchet. Meanwhile, another shadowy figure was coming up the alleyway from the other direction. The two figures came together and seemed to use sign language to one another. They then climbed the pipes and, as they reached the rooftops in Cambridge Street, one of them threw a firecracker down to the victim. The exploding firework distracted the policeman and sent him running towards the murder victim and the two masked men took the opportunity to escape down another pipe into Mulberry Street, where they ran off into the fog. All this took place literally within minutes.

The murder victim was never identified and the woman who witnessed the well-planned slaying was moved to another part of the city by the police because they feared reprisals from the mysterious masked killers. An oriental expert who studied the case believed the murder victim had been slain by Ninja hitmen who had been acting out a classical revenge killing. Just why they killed the victim is still unknown.

The Car from Hell

It is widely assumed that ghosts are spirits of the dead yet there have been thousands of reports of ghostly inanimate objects over the years, such as phantom houses and vehicles. For example, from 1975 to the present day, there have been around thirty separate reports of a phantom bus which runs along Liverpool's Grove Street long after all the bus services have ceased. The phantom vehicle is an old green and white single-decker number 25 bus and it has the destination Penny Lane on its front. The interior of the solid-looking bus is always blazing with light but there is never any sign of a driver or passenger. Most of the people who have seen the ghost-bus over the years have been policemen who have chased the vehicle as it jumps sets of traffic lights between Brownlow Hill and Mulgrave Street. One morning at 2.40am, a policeman who saw the bus thought someone had stolen the outdated-looking vehicle from the depot. He chased the single-decker to Mulgrave Street, where he was shocked to see it fade away before his eyes. The policeman was later relieved to hear from colleagues that he was not going insane; he had merely witnessed the so-called 'Grove Street Ghost-Bus'.

There is another phantom vehicle that patrols the streets of Liverpool from dusk till dawn, mostly during the winter, and this is a frightening and dangerous apparition known as 'The Car from Hell'.

The car is a white Ford Capri which roars along Upper Parliament Street and the area round the Dock Road. It was most active in the late 1970s when the Merseyside Police were constantly chasing the vehicle which showed the same disregard to a red traffic light as the Grove Street Ghost-Bus. At least four police cars have crashed chasing the Hell-car but, unlike the ghost-bus, a grotesque skeletal driver has been seen at the wheel of the spectral Capri.

In 1979 the Capri chased a couple in a Cortina who were returning from a day out in Blackpool. When the Capri zoomed past the Cortina, missing the car by inches, the Cortina driver made the mistake of putting two fingers up to the mad motorist. The Capri decelerated until it was parallel with the Cortina and only then did the couple realise that the driver of the Capri was either in very bad health, or he was wearing a Halloween skeleton mask. The couple in the car shuddered when they saw that the Capri driver had the head of a skeleton and pink glassy-looking eyes. His jaws opened as if he was laughing as he spun his steering wheel in a suicidal manner. The Capri cut right across the lane and the path of the Cortina. The Cortina driver swerved to avoid what seemed to be an imminent collision and hit the kerb. The front tyre of the Cortina burst as it sheared against the kerb and the car spun around. Seconds later, the Capri literally disappeared into thin air about a hundred yards down the road, leaving the Cortina driver and his wife in a state of shock.

When the police arrived at the scene, the Cortina driver told them about the insane manoeuvres of the Capri driver. He expected the police to doubt his story about the maniac wearing a Halloween mask but the police reacted in a strange, quiet way, as if they had heard such reports before.

A week later, at 5 o'clock in the morning, the Capri and its ghoulish-looking driver chased a Royal Mail lorry from Copperas Hill. The driver of the mail lorry looked in his side mirrors and thought a masked criminal was following the vehicle, ready to ambush him. He stepped on the gas but the Capri disappeared behind the lorry. Then something incredible happened; the Capri reappeared as a speck of light coming from the other direction on the wrong side of the road. The lorry driver had to think fast, and he performed a dangerous manoeuvre by turning sharply down a side street as the Capri whizzed by. The driver of the mail lorry left his vehicle and ran to the top of the street to see if he could get a look at the Capri's registration but, as he looked down the road, his hair stood on end. The Capri started to fade away in the dawn light until it was just a faint smudge of light moving down Sefton Street. A colleague of the mailman at Copperas Hill later told him that he had seen the 'Dock Road Ghost-Car' which had even been reported in the *Daily Post*.

In 1980, workmen clearing up the Albert Dock dredged up a white Ford Capri buried deep under the mud and silt of the dock. There were rumours at the time that the car wreckage contained the skeleton of a joyrider who had crashed the vehicle purposely into the dock in an act of suicide. Police were baffled by the find, as no one had seen the car plunging into the dock. They surmised that the vehicle had been driven into the water in the early hours of the morning but they would not speculate on the fate of the Capri driver. Several workmen said they had seen a skeleton in tattered clothes falling out of a Capri into the muddy waters of the dock. Was the corpse the decomposed driver of the ghostly Capri car?

Shopping Mall Ghosts

The following weird incidents happened in a certain shopping mall on Merseyside.

Tony, a security guard, was looking at a bank of monitors in the closed-circuit TV room of a shopping mall. At around three o'clock in the morning, he saw a figure moving across screen five, which covered the parking area outside. A dark-haired man in a blue shirt walked across the screen towards Tony's car, then went down on his knees and collapsed face down. Tony was not allowed to leave the monitor room, so he radioed two other guards who were patrolling the mall and alerted them. Within a minute, the two guards were at the car park but there was no sign of anybody on the floor near Tony's car. The two guards double checked and patrolled the car park twice, looking under their own cars and shining their torches into the vehicles. The mystery man was nowhere to be seen.

Tony was shocked to see that the figure had gone from his monitor and really thought that a car thief was at large. The image had looked so real. However, when Tony got permission to rewind the security tape, there was no image of the man in the parking lot, just a curious amount of interference in the form of flickering horizontal lines.

The following Monday morning, again at 3am, Tony casually glanced up and saw the same eerie figure in a blue shirt walking across the screen. Again, the man sank to his knees and fell forward onto his face. Tony alerted his colleagues and, this time, he left the monitor room and rushed down to the car park, determined to catch the man. As he yanked open the heavy fire door to leave the building, a gust of wind blew his cap off. Tony did not pick it up but hurried to the car park to catch the prowler.

When Tony's friends arrived at the spot where the man had been seen to fall, they saw a body lying face down on the tarmac near Tony's car. The man on the floor was Tony; he had had a massive heart attack and had died almost instantly. The guards later talked about the strange and tragic incident and one of them said what both of them had been thinking; had Tony been seeing sneak-previews of his own death on the security monitor?

Many more strange images have been seen on the monitors of the closed-circuit TV room, including the shadowy figure of a woman walking through the shopping mall in the early hours of the morning. She is believed to be the ghost of a woman who owned a shop at the mall. She died in a car crash on her way back from work five years ago. She has even waved to the security cameras. Five months ago, one guard, who did not know the mall was haunted, left his job after seeing the ghostly pale face of a smiling woman on all of the security monitors.

Last Dance

There is a church in Liverpool's Edge Hill district that was once the setting of a tragic romance. The man and woman in this long-forgotten drama were Olivia Stroud, a beautiful porcelain-skinned girl of twenty-one, and her childhood sweetheart James Divine, a soldier.

Olivia and James were both born in Marmaduke Street within days of each other in 1899. They lived next door to each other and had been the best of friends. At fourteen, they had both fallen in love and had both vowed to marry one day. Sadly, the First World War had intervened and James returned from the infamous Battle of the Somme a changed man. His grim first-hand experiences of the futile carnage of the War had made the young man turn to drink and transformed him into a sarcastic troublemaker. Yet, in her heart, Olivia knew that in James' troubled soul there were traces of the boy she knew so well and loved.

In 1920, a dance was held at the church in Durning Road and James turned up with a few of his old comrades from the War. Several times, Olivia asked him to dance with her but James always replied, "No, I'll join you at the last dance," and continued drinking with his friends.

Olivia's beauty was legendary in the district and she was known as 'The Belle of Edge Hill'. Today, Olivia would undoubtedly have been snapped up by Hollywood. She was not only extraordinarily attractive but also had a mysterious, beguiling charisma. All the young men sighed as she took to the floor with an elderly man who had dared to ask her to dance. James just stood at the makeshift bar with a sarcastic look on his face as Olivia, dressed in a beautiful lace gown, waltzed by. By midnight, James was fairly intoxicated and the sentimental boy Olivia once knew started to show through the soldier's tough but false front. As James watched Olivia walk towards him, he felt his heart burn with sorrow. He should have danced with her earlier, instead of humouring his old mates. Something deep down told him that there would never be another night like this and he reached out to his childhood sweetheart with open arms as a crowd of jealous men looked on.

Suddenly, Olivia stopped smiling and stood still. She bowed her head and looked drowsy.

"Olivia – what's wrong?" James rushed over to her.

Olivia seemed dizzy and fell down onto the wooden panelled floor of the church hall. The colour started to drain from her beautiful face.

"James, I don't feel well. Take me home."

"Olivia! Somebody please get a doctor," cried James, with a look of frantic horror.

He picked up the girl and lifted her in his arms but did not know what to do. An old grey-haired man rushed from the crowd and said he was a doctor. He told James to lay the girl on the floor and took her pulse, then felt her forehead. The doctor diagnosed that she had a fever of some sort.

Olivia was taken home to Marmaduke Street and became delirious. She kept saying "James, what about the last dance? Why wouldn't you dance with me?"

At one in the morning, Olivia stopped breathing and quietly died. James cried unashamedly over the body of his first and last love and squeezed her hand tightly.

The postmortem revealed that Olivia had been poisoned in a most bizarre way. The girl's parents had recently fallen on hard times and had bought a secondhand dress from a tailor in London Road for her to wear at the dance. The tailor had obtained the lace dress from an undertaker who later confessed that he had taken it from the body of a girl prior to her burial. That girl had been embalmed, and the dress she had worn had soaked up a quantity of the poisonous embalming fluid. The fluid had seeped out of the dress and soaked through the pores of Olivia's skin as she danced, slowly poisoning her. James drove himself insane and literally drank himself into an early grave.

In 1942, an ARP warden was patrolling Edge Hill during a blackout, when he saw a faint light in a church. Entering the church, he saw that the light was radiating from the ghostly figure of a young lady in a white dress who was walking across the hall with her head bowed. Even today, the ghost of the tragic Olivia is still seen, walking across the church hall, perhaps always waiting in vain for the last dance with her long-dead sweetheart.

The Haunted Man

According to an old Irish proverb, 'A guilty conscience needs no accuser,' and the following true story is about the conscience of a killer's mind.

It is said that 'the criminal always returns to the scene of the crime.' In the year 1855, Henry Arkle, a forty-year-old timber merchant, bumped into Charles Wilson, a window cleaner, in Liverpool's Dale Street. Arkle had lent the window cleaner money five months previously to pay off a gambling debt and Wilson still had not paid a farthing of it back to the merchant. Arkle grabbed the window cleaner by the lapels of his coat and shook him demanding, "You'll pay up some of the money you owe me – now!"

Wilson said he would pay on Friday when he had collected his wages and explained that he had not been feeling well recently because he had been suffering from food poisoning.

Friday came and went and Charlie Wilson did not pay his debt, so Henry Arkle decided to settle the matter in a cowardly and violent way. At that time in Liverpool, the poor had been rioting because the harvest had been disastrous. Flour and wheat were being sold at a premium. One morning, a terrible riot broke out and shops and bakeries were plundered by the hungry mob. Henry Arkle got caught up in the middle of one of these riots and, in the middle of the turmoil, saw Charlie Wilson hurling a coping-stone through a baker's window. Arkle pulled down his hat till it covered his eyes and pushed through the crowd. When he was behind Wilson, who was urging the rioters to steal the bread, he reached into his boot and pulled out a short dagger called a dirk, which had been given to him by his Scottish uncle. Arkle glanced around and, seeing that the mob were too preoccupied with raiding the bakery to notice, plunged the dagger into Wilson's back. He stabbed him again and again as he cheered on the rioters in the deafening din. Wilson turned around slowly, spluttering up the blood from his punctured lungs. He had the terrible expression of a man who knows he is about to die as he looked Arkle in the eye and asked, "Why?"

Henry Arkle burned with guilt, and shoved the stabbed window cleaner to the floor, where he was trampled by the mob of men and women as they rushed towards the bakery. The police made enquiries but the killer of Charles Wilson could not be found, so the authorities surmised that the window cleaner had been accidentally killed by the mob.

At midnight a month later, an old woman called at Arkle's house off Mount Pleasant and claimed she had seen him repeatedly knife Wilson in the back during the riot. She demanded £100 and warned him that if he did not comply she would go straight to the police. Should he try to harm her, the old woman confidently promised that her husband would go straight to the police.

Henry Arkle had an excellent memory and he knew the old woman was just a poor match-seller who lived on her own in Roscoe Street. He had seen her many times and knew she was lying about having a husband. He pretended to go and fetch the blackmailer her money but picking up his dagger instead, he cut her throat.

He locked his doors and decapitated the woman with a hacksaw, planning to throw the unidentifiable and headless body into the Liverpool to Leeds canal. Arkle put some more coal and wood on the fire, then placed the old woman's head on it. The grey hair singed and ignited and the flames turned the flesh black. The stench was terrible and the heat had a strange effect on the head, causing the eyelids to shoot open. The eyes looked at the horrified merchant with an accusing stare. Arkle screamed out and thrust the glowing poker into one of the eyeballs and it popped, showering him with a vile watery fluid.

At 3am, the merchant carted the headless naked body of the old woman to the Liverpool and Leeds canal near Vauxhall Road and dumped it in. It was tied to three heavy stones, so plunged into the waters with a loud splash. Arkle waited as the ripples radiated across the waters of the canal, as the body submerged. Returning home, Henry Arkle saw to his horror that the one-eyed head of the blackmailer just would not burn, so he buried it in the small garden in front of his house beneath the rockery.

The double murderer finally got to bed around 5am. Shortly after falling asleep, the dreams began. He dreamt of the old woman's head on the fire and when her eyes would open he would awake with a scream. Another distressing dream pricked at his conscience. He felt himself rising up out of his bed and, after floating out the window, he would fly across the rooftops until he was hovering over the moonlit cemetery in Church Alley, off Church Street. Then Arkle would start to descend down towards a pauper's grave marked with a little stone marker. He knew this was the grave of the window cleaner he had stabbed because he had visited that grave many times out of guilt to pray for forgiveness. In the nightmare, Arkle would descend through the cold soil and clay until he was in the coffin with his murder victim. The dream ended with the murder victim saying, "I'm still alive. Please dig me up, Henry! I'm still alive!" and Charlie Wilson would then start to scream and scratch at the coffin lid until his fingernails were dripping with blood. Wilson would become hysterical and he would start to smash his forehead against the coffin lid as he tried in vain to get out the claustrophobic box. Henry Arkle woke up at this point, soaked in sweat, his heart pounding in his ears.

These horrific nightmares haunted Henry Arkle for weeks. The merchant's business suffered, and he slowly descended into insanity and became bankrupt. One morning, he caused a commotion by screaming at a group of pigeons in his front garden. He thought that they were pecking at the remains of the old woman's head that he had buried there but they were just pecking at a small millet plant that had sprung up in the rockery. The bemused neighbours would sneer at him as they watched him constantly peeping out the window of his house at the front garden with a look of dread.

That autumn, Henry Arkle's conscience finally got the better of his warped mind. At three in the morning, he left his house at with a spade and a lantern wrapped in a sack. He looked pale and had black rings around his bloodshot eyes – he had not enjoyed a good night's sleep in months because of all the nightmares. He sneaked down the back streets until he reached the shadows of a church which stood on the site now occupied by the Top Shop store in Church Street. Arkle scaled the railings of the church cemetery and, lighting his lantern, roamed the gravestones until he found the pauper's grave where Charles Wilson had been laid to rest. In the twisted mind of the timber merchant, he really believed that Wilson was still alive in the grave and that, if he could be dug up, the world would see that Henry Arkle was not a murderer.

They say a madman has extra strength and Arkle frantically dug and spaded away like a machine. Not once did he stop. At last his spade hit the lid of the coffin. He sighed, "It won't be long now, Mr Wilson," and started to smash the lid of the cheaply made coffin to splinters with the spade. The racket alerted a policeman who was patrolling nearby and he went to investigate the source of the noise. Climbing over the gates of the cemetery, he saw the lantern by edge of the open grave. Peering into the deep hole, he saw Henry Arkle shaking the decomposing body of his murder victim. Wriggling worms fell out of the eye sockets and teeth of the corpse as Arkle screamed "No! You're not dead! You told me to dig you up! You can't be dead!"

The policeman blew hard on his whistle and alerted his colleagues. Arkle was taken to the bridewell in Cheapside and made a full confession about the two murders. After taking the statements from him, the recording officer told everyone to get some sleep, as a proper hearing would resume in the morning. Arkle was put in his cell but, as usual, did not sleep a wink. He probably never rested until he hung from the end of the hangman's rope a month later.

Hell House

Somewhere in the north west there is an unremarkable Victorian terraced house. Many readers will have passed it without giving it a second glance but, since the year 1900, this innocent-looking dwelling has been dubbed the 'Hell House' for reasons I will relate to you.

In 1900, the owner of the house, Dr Edward Meade, died and left it to Oliver Milton, his wayward eighteen-year-old nephew. He was known as a bounder and a hellraiser who, although still a teenager, had four illegitimate children in Liverpool, Preston, Chester and Northwich. It is recorded that in 1898, when Oliver was just sixteen, he acted as a referee to a duel between two farmers at a field outside Cuddington. He was accused of putting a blank in the pistol of the farmer who died and it later transpired that Oliver had received a substantial payment to tamper with the pistol.

In 1899, Oliver decided with a group of like-minded friends to make a pact with the Devil on Bidston Hill on the Wirral. Upon a sandstone outcrop by Bidston Observatory, Oliver and his companions summoned up Lucifer with a chant they had learned from an old man in Wales who had professed to be a black magician. The sandstone rock on Bidston was said to have been a traditional place for magical rites for over a thousand years. There are still strange carvings on the rock of a cat-headed Moon goddess and a horse.

According to Oliver, the Devil materialised just after midnight as a man in black with a charming voice. He said that if the young men swore allegiance to him they would all have great careers and he asked them to raise their arms to salute him with their open palms. This sounds like the black magic sign that Hitler adopted many years later as the Nazi salute.

The man in black then smiled and faded away.

Weird things then began to happen to him and his friends. They had tremendous runs of luck when gambling and became very popular with girls but there were always reminders of their pact with Satan. One Welsh girl bore one of the boys an illegitimate girl and, when the midwife examined her, the baby had a birthmark on her back which looked exactly like a three-pronged fork. Another of the boys left the gang and tried to settle down to marry a girl in Wrexham but when he entered the church for the wedding ceremony, he became violently ill. The girl and the villagers became suspicious. The priest pushed the teenager into the church and barred his way out. The boy took a fit and rolled across the floor of the aisle, frothing at the mouth. He then got to his feet, pushed three strong men aside, fled from the church and left Wrexham and the broken-hearted bride-to-be.

Oliver had no intentions of marrying and settled in the house left to him by his Uncle Edward. The servants were kept on and Oliver begrudgingly paid them a meagre wage from the fortune his uncle had left him. The teenager gave specific instructions to the staff that no one must go into the cellar when he was down there or they would be instantly dismissed. Everyone agreed to this bizarre stipulation except a young maid, Polly, who had a reputation for being very nosey. Her curiosity got the better of her one stormy night when Oliver took a lantern down to the cellar and locked himself in. Hearing a strange chant, Polly left her kitchen duties and sneaked down into the cellar and spied on Oliver through a slit in the cellar door. What she saw made her speechless with fear. Oliver was kneeling on the floor and chanting in a weird voice. Suddenly a tall man in black with a pale child-like face appeared. The figure's eyes seemed to burn with a golden light. Oliver said to the apparition, "I've had it with you. I want no more from you. I reject you, Lucifer! Your promises are always hollow and full of snags."

The man's face broke into a smile.

"You swore allegiance and you're mine forever; mind, body, and soul."

"No!" shouted Oliver and he getting up off his knees, took a swipe at the man but his arm went through him.

"I've had enough of your turncoat ways. I'm taking you away tonight!" the stranger announced and then vanished, leaving a terrible stench behind.

Polly stood on a creaking step as she tried to run up the stairs in the dark. Oliver heard her, chased after her and seized her.

"Polly, did you see what went on down there?" he demanded

The girl nodded, and started to sob.

"Please help me, Polly. He said he'll take me tonight."

"I can't," she cried and she ran upstairs and told the other servants. They were so afraid, they all resigned at once and left the house in a hurry. The local clergyman was told about Oliver's secret meetings with Satan, and he visited the house the following morning with two other priests, intending to perform an exorcism. There was no answer at the house, so they got a policeman to gain entry by breaking the door open. Up in the bedroom, everyone could smell something burning. The policeman lifted the bedclothes and there were the charred remains of Oliver Milton. The blackened remains were so small, they looked like a piece of burnt toast. The policeman noted that there was a black powder on the bedsheets and a single blackened foot at the bottom of the mattress. Yet neither the bedclothes nor the bed were even singed. The pathologist surmised that Oliver Milton had been a victim of what is known as spontaneous human combustion, where the body heat of a person rises to such intensity it is consumed by an intense fire.

Polly knew that was not the explanation. She told the police that Lucifer had paid a visit to one of his disciples and taken him from his bed. The police just sneered at her story. It is said that within the house where Oliver practised his black arts, terrible screams are still heard and foul, sulphuric smells occasionally rise up from the cellar.

As recently as 1996, workmen at the house saw the word 'Mammon' being chalked on a wall by an invisible hand. Mammon is mentioned in the Bible as the god of money and greed. One resident who lived in the house of horror with his family said that the foundations of the dwelling seemed to vibrate and give off a groaning sound whenever the bells of the local church rang out on Sundays. A couple from Manchester who lived at the Merseyside house in the late 1960s left the spooky dwelling because each morning when they awoke, they would find that their double bed had been rotated 180 degrees ...

The Shakespeare Curse

Actors are renowned for their superstitions; they wish each other luck by saying "Break a leg" and call Shakespeare's Macbeth "the Scottish Play". Even someone whistling on a stage is thought to invite bad luck in dramatic circles. Worse still is the thought of a jinxed theatre and many performers over the years have suspected the Shakespeare Theatre that once stood in Liverpool's Fraser Street.

The Shakespeare Theatre was opened on 27 August 1888 with a production of *As You Like It*. During rehearsals for the play, an actor dropped dead on stage. The coroner recorded death by natural causes but the actor was only twenty-seven and seemed to have been in the best of health. He was even teetotal. Not long afterwards, phantom sounds of someone sobbing were frequently heard coming from the wings, and, late one evening, a troupe of actors became alarmed when they heard someone marching heavily across the stage.

In January 1889, the manager hammered on a dressing room door, demanding to see an actor who owed him money. The door opened and a hand passed out a piece of blank paper, then slammed the door in the manager's face. The manager and an old man who operated the limelight resorted to forcing the door open but were shocked to find the dressing room empty. The actor who owed the money turned up at the theatre later that evening, saying he did not feel too well. The following morning, he was found dead in his bed at a Lime Street hotel. In the early 1900s, a painter was decorating the auditorium, when something pushed the ladder he was on. The decorator fell, almost breaking his neck and he refused to finish the job because he claimed he had heard a whispering voice coming from the stage.

A Catholic priest was brought in to perform an exorcism. The comedian Rob Wilton, who was making his debut at the theatre, thought the whole ghost thing was ridiculous. However, one afternoon when Wilton and several other performers were rehearsing a play, a spotlight switched itself on and its beam swept the stage, even though there was no one up in the rigging at the time.

An even more chilling incident took place the following week, when clapping from the auditorium interrupted the rehearsal of a tragedy scene. The leading actress let out a scream. She said she saw a pair of pale ghostly hands clapping away as they floated above one of the seats. A couple of days later, a phantom heckler kept booing another rehearsal session and brought the production to a standstill.

An impromptu séance was held on stage in an effort to get to the bottom of the supernatural distractions. The glass spelt out the word 'Fire' – then splintered dramatically. Pieces of glass flew in different directions and an icy breeze blew across the stage. In the following weeks, strange burning smells alarmed the cast and audience on several occasions. Nobody knew it at the time, but some five hundred years before, several women accused of witchcraft and sorcery were burnt at the stake on the site occupied by the theatre. Could all the spooky activity have had something to do with the execution of the witches?

Fire certainly featured prominently in the history of the theatre. In the 1940s. The Blitz brought the curtain down on the 'Shakey', as it was affectionately known. It re-opened after the war only to close again, in March 1956. The theatre had been continually dogged by financial troubles. The American actor, Sam Wanamaker, stepped in and funded several productions of Tennessee Williams' plays and it opened once more. The Shakey still ended up in the red and financial support from an American heiress named Anna Deere Winman was withdrawn. Miss Winman later died after a fall at her Bermuda home and many thought that the ugly curse had reared its head once more.

The theatre was resurrected once again, in November 1963, as a luxurious night spot featuring cabaret, a dance hall and even a casino but, just a fortnight after opening, the Shakespeare was gutted by a blaze. Three years later over £175,000 was spent rebuilding the theatre and, once more, the curtain went up. This time the theatre had a stylish, ultra-extravagant interior which was probably the only one of its kind in Europe. There was a Mexican bar, a South Sea Island bar and a sixty foot long Promenade Bar situated in the auditorium. For the next decade, the Shakey featured a galaxy of stars and was fronted by Peter Price, outrageous camp compere. Stars including Johnny Ray, Tommy Cooper, Freddie Starr, Olivia Newton John, Sacha Distel, Frankie Vaughan and Dorothy Squires appeared but, on 21 March, 1976, the theatre was completely wrecked by another fire. This time the final curtain came down and The Liverpool City Council Surveyor condemned the burnt-out shell as unsafe and it was later demolished. Why was the theatre dogged by so much misfortune and strange goings-on? Was it all coincidence – or was the theatre cursed by some malevolent supernatural force?

The Legend of Mary Crane

There is an old proverb, "Speak of the Devil and he'll appear". That saying is a throwback to an old belief in the power of spoken magic or spells, as we call them.

This final tale concerns a witch who was greatly feared by a community in the picturesque setting of the Forest of Bowland. Even today, the mere mention of the Witch of Bowland Forest is greeted with an uneasy silence in a certain Lancashire tavern. An old legend says that the eyes of her corpse will fly open in her grave if her name is so much as uttered. So be very careful, not to speak her name, for she will rise from her grave and come to haunt you ...

In December 1812, three woodcutters from the village of Abbeystead, which lies seven miles south-east of Lancaster, were instructed by Lord Trenchard to bring an enormous fir tree from the Forest of Bowland. The Lord had selected the tree and had chalked a white cross upon its bark. The woodcutters were to chop the tree down and cart it back to Abbeystead. It seemed a simple enough task. The woodcutters reached the forest after making a detour to an old friend who made his own cider, so by the time they reached the forest, they were quite drunk. One waved a hatchet and the other two carried a long saw and they sang as they rolled along the path into the dense forest.

The oldest woodcutter, a well-built man named John Perry, spotted the white cross on the huge fir tree. He saw to his dismay that it was almost 40 feet in height. That meant that the men would have to haul the tree onto the cart and have it drawn back to the village by their two old shire horses; a daunting task. The three men set about sawing through the hard trunk of the fir but it was very thirsty work. Perry told his workmates, two young twins, Norman and Daniel, to have a go at sawing through the tree, but they too found the task demanding. After a while, young Norman pointed to a clearing,

"Look. Someone lives there. They might spare us a drink and some food."

A quaint-looking little wooden house stood in the shadows of the forest. It was crudely built, little more than a shanty. When a young woman in her twenties, with long black hair, emerged from the hut carrying a basket, the three men smiled and, as she passed by, old Mr Perry tipped his hat, "Good day to ye, Miss."

But the woman just looked the men up and down and walked on. She went over to the base of a tree, picked some toadstools, put them in her basket and walked off into the forest. When she was out of sight, Mr Perry said, "My, she was a pretty maiden. Let us see if her family's at home."

They went over to the hut and peeped through the window. There was no sign of anybody in there, so the men pulled open the door and entered. The intruders soon realised that they had entered the home of a witch. A small cauldron hung on a chain over a flickering fire and, on the hearth-stone near the grate, was a human skull, probably unearthed from Abbeystead graveyard. Hanging from one of the crossbeams of the low ceiling was a collection of little effigies made from rags and real human hair with pins stuck in them.

One of the twins picked up a book and flipped through its pages. There were detailed drawings of plants with notes scribbled under the diagrams. Then Perry noticed a small round table with a black cloth upon it. Picking up the cloth, he revealed a large egg-shaped piece of clear polished amber.

"What the deuce is that?" asked one of the twins.

"Some type of crystal ball, I imagine," replied Perry.

Suddenly, they recoiled in horror as the faint image of a blue eye appeared in the amber and stared back at them. The three ran out of the house in terror.

After they had recovered from the shock, Perry remarked "It must be the house of Mary Crane." The mere mention of the name made them all shiver. What happened next is not too clear but Mary Crane saw the men coming from her house as she returned from the forest. She dropped her basket and raised her hands to the men, as if she was about to cast some evil spell on them. Daniel ran off in a state of terror and did not stop until he reached the village of Abbeystead.

He returned to the clearing with a mob but there was no sign of

Mary Crane, or Mr Perry and his brother Norman. Then, one of the villagers pointed to the fir tree marked with a cross. There, nailed to its trunk, were the bodies of old Mr Perry and Norman. The men had been nailed to the tree with long iron spikes that penetrated their foreheads and necks.

The vicar of Abbeystead then stirred up the mob by crying out:

"See what this agent of the Devil has done! Mary Crane will be hanged for this crime, for it is written in the scriptures: 'Thou shalt not suffer a witch to live!' Find her and kill her!"

A strange twilight fell on the forest and the temperature plunged until the cold was unbearable. The mob hurried back along the road to Abbeystead and, during their retreat, the sound of a woman cackling could be heard nearby. A strange, large black cat leapt out of a tree and attacked the vicar. The overgrown feline seized his head and clawed one of his eyes out of its socket. The mob, in a panic, stampeded back to the village.

The following morning, just after sunrise, a larger mob returned to the little wooden house of Mary Crane and tried to set fire to it with torches and buckets of tar, yet the wooden dwelling refused to burn. The mob resorted to smashing up the house with hatchets, then returned to the village. That night, the beer in the tavern turned sour and several farm animals dropped dead for no apparent reason. At the first stroke of midnight, the barmaid at the tavern screamed and clutched at her face. The red, blistering imprint of a hand slowly appeared on her cheek and the impression never went away and she was scarred for life.

On Christmas Eve, two travellers from Lancaster came down a country road to Abbeystead to visit their relatives for Christmas and observed a crowd of people dressed in white walking in the moonlight on the edge of Bowland Forest. One of the travellers thought the figures were ghosts and wanted to ride away but his companion persuaded him to take a closer look at the nocturnal activity. They rode into the forest and what they saw sent a shiver down their spines. The people were wearing nightgowns and nightdresses and seemed to be in a trance. It was almost as if they were all sleepwalking. But these sleepwalkers were carrying out tasks under the supervision of a young woman dressed in black. As the fascinated travellers came nearer to the bizarre scene, they recognised four of their own relatives among the fifty-odd crowd. The group was building a new home for the woman on the other side of the forest and the travellers realised with dread that the weird taskmaster was Mary Crane. One of the travellers produced a pistol and fired at the witch and she shrieked, running off into the forest, followed by a large black cat.

At that precise moment, all the somnambulists awoke from their trance and were puzzled to find themselves in the forest. The last thing they remembered was going to bed. The villagers requested the services of a professional witch-hunter and some six months later, an old man rode into Abbeystead. He was George Mandeville and he convinced Lord Trenchard that he had the skill to rid the scared villagers of the witch. Mandeville used a dowsing rod to track her down and he and a group of armed villagers encircled Mary Crane with salt and captured her.

She was hanged the same day and Mandeville had her buried face-down beneath a certain crossroads near the village. He then ordered the villagers not to even breathe one mention of her name, warning that each mention of Mary Crane would give her spirit more and more strength to return to life with a vengeance. The villagers obeyed Mandeville's advice, but one particular villager wrote the story down and committed it to posterity. So now that you have read this story, please do not repeat it and talk of you-know-who; or she might just pay you a visit.

OTHER TITLES
Published by The Bluecoat Press

Available from all good bookshops
For a free stocklist contact
The Bluecoat Press, 45 Bluecoat Chambers, School Lane, Liverpool L1 3BX
Telephone 0151 707 2390

If you have had a paranormal encounter,
or a supernatural experience of any sort, please drop a line to:

Thomas Slemen
c/o The Bluecoat Press
45 Bluecoat Chambers
School Lane
Liverpool L1 3BX

All correspondence will be answered.